G000152382

Cakes

MARY NORWAK

A BOOK OF BEST BRITISH RECIPES

Illustrations by Prue Theobalds

B T BATSFORD LTD · *LONDON*

Printer's Error
The second line of the method for **Coffee Fudge Cake** should read:
oven to 400°F/200°C/Gas Mark 6. Whisk the eggs, sugar and coffee

Now stir the fire, and close the shutters fast,
Let fall the curtains, wheel the sofa round,
And, while the bubbling and loud-hissing urn
Throws up a steady column, and the cups,
That cheer but not inebriate, wait on each,
So let us welcome peaceful evening in. . . .

(William Cowper)

First published 1984

ISBN 0 7134 41046

Typeset by Deltatype, Ellesmere Port, South Wirral
Printed and bound in Great Britain by
Biddles Ltd
Guildford and King's Lynn
for the publishers
B. T. Batsford Ltd.
4 Fitzhardinge Street
London W1H 0AH

Contents

Introduction 7

1 The Story of British Cakes 9
2 Ingredients, Equipment and Methods 14
3 Griddlecakes, Scones and Potato Cakes 21
4 Yeastcakes and Buns 34
5 Gingerbreads, Honey Cakes and Spice Cakes 53
6 Fruit Cakes and Fruit Loaves 69
7 Cut-and-Come-Again Cakes 95
8 Sponge Cakes 109
9 Special Occasion Cakes 116
10 Pastry Cakes and Tarts 126
11 Small Cakes 137
12 Biscuits and Fairings 147
13 Icings and Pastry 166

British/American Conversion Tables 171
Index 174

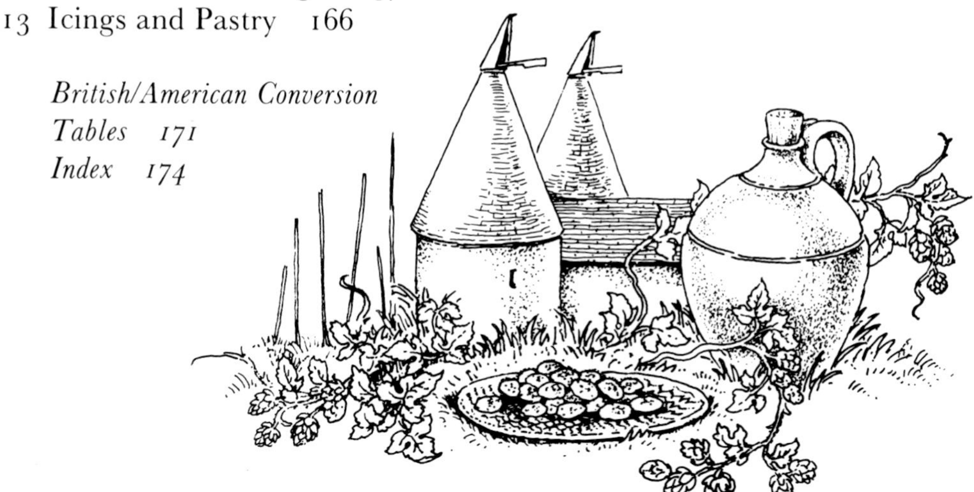

Introduction

And the colour of that spicy cake came back upon my recollection and the pleasure and the curiosity I had taken in seeing her make it.

(Charles Lamb)

No other food in history seems to have had the same effect on the 'recollection' as cake. Marcel Proust's small, spongy, shell-shaped madeleine stimulated his *Remembrance of Times Past* and inspired his great series of novels. Which of us has not sometimes paused to remember the milestones of life and their accompanying cakes? Our pagan ancestors welcomed the seasons with fires and sacrifices and ceremonial cakes, and throughout the world people of all races and creeds still mark seasons, festivals and personal celebrations by an appropriate sweetmeat.

In Britain many of us begin the celebrations with a christening cake, traditionally the top layer of the wedding cake, richly fruited and iced. Already my memory stirs because a quarter of a century ago we broke with tradition and gave my eldest daughter's godparents and guests a great cartwheel of a gâteau from a Soho patisserie, the sponge layers soaked in rum and covered with a soft white icing, lavishly sprinkled with sugared violets. In childhood, our birthdays are marked by the ingenuity of trains and castles, cats and houses, and the popularity of the party can be judged by the consumption or rejection of the cake. My mother, one of ten children, and now nearly ninety, remembers how her mother forgot to make a cake to greet her return from school after a three-mile walk on her sixth birthday, but compensated by making a huge pile of pancakes instead.

We proceed to the fantastic edifice of the wedding cake, often dry with rock-hard icing, but a symbol of yet another milestone in life, and the little boxed pieces sent to absent friends and family truly indicate that we have taken a drastic step. In some parts of Britain the funeral cake still flourishes, packaged in a gloomy wrapper which represents life's misfortunes and ultimate end. From cradle to grave we mark the seasons with Christmas Cake, Simnel Cake and Hot Cross Buns, Guy Fawkes' Parkin, Black Bun and shortbread. As we travel we can still enjoy the regional specialities of Cornish Saffron Cake, Eccles and Banbury Cakes, Norfolk Fair Buttons and Northumberland Singin' Hinnies. On happy holidays we pause for tea and scones, and on miserable days we console ourselves with chocolate cake.

In everyday life tea is the only meal which is now relaxed and friendly. Breakfast, if eaten at all, is hurried and often eaten in tense silence. The lunch break may be the time for a scrambled shopping expedition, an indigestible and worrying business meeting with too much wine and too many calories, or a solitary snack of fish fingers for the housebound. The evening meal may be a snatched supper on the way to some adult learning, a committee meeting or an entertainment; or it may be a formal return-match dinner party with everyone on best behaviour and the cook-hostess tense with worry about food and incompatible guests. Only teatime remains as the gentle timeless meal to which we invite our nicest and most gossipy friends. Whoever looks back with real pleasure on a dinner party? But how many of us remember the 4 o'clock rest in the garden, the snug Sunday tea by the fire, the beach or country picnic, or the matey cuppa and fattening biscuits in a friend's kitchen?

It is hardly surprising that housewives of earlier centuries filled their handwritten cookery books with cake recipes, and that later printed books had the cake recipes in the first chapter. Few friends want to share their cunning ways with stews and roasts, and perhaps there is little to share in such recipes. But there is a good deal to share in delectable cakes, those remembrancers of happy times, and I hope that you will enjoy sharing my collection of traditional and regional goodies left by my ancestors and many other good housewives whose pride was in their kitchens and whose happiness was in the gatherings of their families.

1 *The Story of British Cakes*

> When I left school I worked at the village bakehouse for a time, and rather enjoyed it. I soon learnt to 'set sponge' and to mould loaves, but the job I liked best was mixing cakes. The baker's wife examined my hands, arms and fingernails most carefully and made me scrub them till every speck of dirt had vanished; then the ingredients were measured out; so many eggs, so many pounds of fresh butter from the farm, flour, sugar, fruit, etc. The eggs were cracked into a huge bowl, and I used to spend an hour or so mixing, with the eggs and butter squelching through my fingers. Finally, those cakes, quite sizeable ones too, were sold for sixpence, and the villagers grumbled at the price. I wonder how many eggs and pounds of butter they put in the cakes there now?
>
> (C. H. Middleton, *A Village Boyhood*)

Mr Middleton, later to become a famous gardening broadcaster, was writing in the late 1930s of his memories of a village childhood, expressing that wonderful feeling of making a cake. The British have always been renowned for a national sweet tooth and cakes have been popular fare for centuries, although until comparatively recent times they were bought rather than prepared at home, because of the difficulties of preparing ingredients and of baking over an open fire. Daniel Defoe described the way in which a pastrycook's shop was set up in 1710 at a cost of £300. There were sash windows with 'looking-glass' plates, tiles all round the walls of the shop and preparation area painted with forest scenes and figures, and the shop was decorated with looking glasses, candlesticks and lanterns, wall sconces, and large silver candelabra. The sweetmeats were displayed on large silver salvers and there were twelve large high stands for the display of small dishes of tarts and jellies. The ceiling was decorated with carving and gilding, and there were china basins and cups. The pastrycook also needed two ovens and a stock of cheesecakes and other delicacies to the cost of £20. This sounds exactly like the best kind of French or Italian teashop where one may indulge in cakes and ices, but the last similar shops died out in Britain soon after the Second World War.

In Europe the old culinary guilds are still maintained, so that bakers will rarely produce anything more than bread, while pastrycooks only display delicate cakes. Until the nineteenth century these two trades were also distinct in Britain, along with confectioners who prepared small sweetmeats, chocolate-makers and comfit-makers, who all pursued a small specialised branch of their trade. It was acceptable for everyone to buy food in the street, so that as well as the individual shops, there were open stalls and itinerant vendors of cakes, biscuits and other sweetmeats.

Home-baking did not become popular until the eighteenth century, when the first enclosed ovens were developed by Count Rumford and Thomas Robinson, replacing the huge open fires, and enabling the domestic cook to control the heat of her oven. Early ovens, which were rare in private houses, were fired with small pieces of wood to a great heat. The fire was then raked out and bread baked at a high temperature. As the oven cooled, enriched breads, biscuits and lighter cakes could be baked, but it was never easy to control the temperature, and 'baking' in most houses was confined to the open griddle suspended over a raging fire (Chapter Three).

Apart from the difficulty of actually baking the cakes it must have been extremely difficult to prepare the basic ingredients well enough to make a finely flavoured or textured cake. Flour had to be dried by the fire and then sieved to remove the bran and chaff. Sugar had to be broken from a huge, hard sugar loaf which might weigh as much as 50 lb (23 kg), and it then had to be further broken down and sieved, and could never have reached the fineness of today's preparation. Honey and treacle were thick and coarse and dried fruit had to be carefully sorted, then washed and completely dried (raisins had to be stoned until the middle of this century). The fat used might be dripping from a joint, or lard from the family pig, while butter might be strongly flavoured, according to the animal fodder used for the milking cows, or might be heavily over-salted or rancid. Marrow from meat bones was often used for the fat content of a cake, and the resulting strong flavours were disguised by orangeflower water, rosewater and spices. The cakes had to be raised by ale yeast, until the eighteenth century began to appreciate the egg as a raising agent, and even then the eggs were small like pullets' eggs and there was no such thing as the graded egg. The modern cook's aids such as self-raising flour, baking powder and golden syrup did not appear in our kitchens until the last half of the eighteenth century, and it is difficult to realise that they have only been in use for a century.

Once the British had found that it was possible to overcome the difficulties of home-baking they developed a great passion for cake as a sweet comforter in all its forms. Their cakes, however, have always remained relatively plain, and specialities do not include the airy and creamy delights of the Continental pastrycook. Our cakes are much simpler, acting as a substitute for bread as a snack or treat, and often associated with a special celebration or religious festival.

The development of teatime as a peculiarly British meal gave a great impetus to cake-making. The main meal of the day in Norman times was served at about 9 a.m. and gradually moved forward until by the eighteenth century it was served at about 2 p.m., although a few old-fashioned institutions such as the universities clung to the earlier hours. People completed their business or indulged in sport during the morning, and then the main meal would continue for anything from four to eight hours, ending in mid-evening with a final course of tea and sweetmeats and cakes.

The development of commerce after the Industrial Revolution at the end of the eighteenth century forced men to leave their homes early in the morning, eat a snack meal around midday and their main meal in the early evening at home. This meant that women were left on their own for long periods, and a light midday meal became popular, but then there was a gap halfway between the two meals and a light snack began to be served around four o'clock, although at the beginning of Queen Victoria's reign this only consisted of thin bread and butter and tea. Cakes which had been served at breakfast (with chocolate), at midday (with Madeira or sherry) or with tea after the evening meal, began to appear during the afternoon break. Women began to be more sociable and the Duchess of Bedford started a fashion for tea-parties attended by idle women and a few dilettante men who did not need to leave home to work.

In the country, and in less fashionable circles, this late afternoon meal became the main meal of the day when the family returned home from school or work, for school meals and office canteens were unknown. The traditional country High Tea developed with its tableful of meats and pies, puddings and tarts, bread, jam and cakes, all washed down with plenty of strong tea. At this meal appetites were hearty, and many regional cakes were enjoyed, as they could be baked in the oven which every house now had and which was continually fired by coal. This kind of hearty tea was taken into the large country houses by the people who came to be servants in the nursery and kitchen, and many men grew up to enjoy a nursery tea after a hard day's work or play.

The passion for cakes was not appreciated by everybody, notably the early Victorian cookery writer Eliza Acton. Unlike most cookery writers who included large chapters on baking in their books, and unlike housewives who recorded more cake recipes than anything else in their commonplace notebooks, Miss Acton was reluctant to include any cake recipes in *Modern Cookery* (1845). Under the heading 'General Remarks on Cakes', she was positively damning about this branch of culinary art:

> We have inserted here but a comparatively limited number of receipts for these 'sweet poisons', as they have been emphatically called, and we would willingly have diminished still further even the space which has been allotted to them, that we might have had room in their stead for others of a more really useful character; but we have felt reluctant to withdraw such a portion of any of the chapters as might materially alter the original character of the work, or cause dissatisfaction to any of our kind readers, we will therefore content ourselves with remarking that more illness is caused by habitual indulgence in the richer and heavier kinds of cakes than could easily be credited by persons who have given no attention to the subject.
>
> Amongst those which have the worse effects are almond and plum pound cakes, as they are called; all varieties of the *brioche* and such others as contain a large quantity of butter and eggs.
>
> The least objectionable are simple buns, biscuits, yeast and sponge cakes, and *meringues*, these last being extremely light and delicate, and made of white of egg and sugar only, are really not unwholesome.

These are strong words indeed, which are echoed today by many cooks and writers, but the popularity of traditional cakes remains, and the home-made variety is so superior to anything which is made commercially that it gives me the greatest pleasure to record the favourite recipes of so many good cooks and hearty eaters. Cake-baking is creative and highly therapeutic and modern cake-makers have nothing to be ashamed of in preparing a food which has retained its popularity for so many centuries.

2 *Ingredients, Equipment and Methods*

Ay, let the pure flour be like the driven snow, bright to the eye, and unadulterate.

(Henry Pickering)

Early cake-making was a rather hit-and-miss affair, when the quality of fat, flour, sugar and fruit could not be guaranteed and measurements were vague. Cakes had to be shaped freehand, or contained in metal hoops, and the primitive oven was a temperamental piece of equipment whose heat could not be efficiently controlled. Today, success can be guaranteed by the use of standard ingredients, by accurate weighing, by a wide range of tins in every shape and size, and by ovens which can be maintained at a set temperature. It is important to follow cake recipes carefully to produce delicious results.

Ingredients

All cake-making ingredients must be fresh and of high quality. Stale flour, eggs and fat can impart most unpleasant flavours to a cake, so if you only indulge in baking at irregular intervals, buy small quantities of ingredients only when needed.

Flour for the recipes in this book should be plain unless otherwise stated, and this is particularly important in rich cake mixtures which need little raising agent. Wholemeal flour may be used for fruitcakes and gingerbreads as a substitute for white flour, but the result will be heavier, dryer and more solid unless more liquid is introduced into the recipe. The same applies to wholemeal pastry, and it is really better to use this flour only for recipes which have been specially formulated for it. Strong plain flour or bread flour is needed for recipes which include yeast. Self-raising flour is used for a few recipes, but was only invented at the end of the last century, so rarely appears in traditional methods.

Baking powder is used to give mixtures a light texture, but **bicarbonate of soda** is the raising agent when honey, treacle and sour milk are used, as it neutralises acids and gives a soft cake.

Sugar will produce varied results, according to the type used. Caster sugar is best for sponge cakes, as it dissolves quickly in whisked and creamed mixtures. Granulated sugar is generally used for plain rubbed-in mixtures and for fruit cakes. Demerara sugar is used for some fruit cakes and biscuits, but it is best to look for natural demerara sugar as some packets contain only coloured refined sugar which lacks the finest flavour. Soft brown sugar may be light or dark and may vary from texture like sand to a sticky toffee texture; the lighter varieties are suitable for plain and fruit cakes, and the darker types give a beautiful flavour to gingerbread. Black treacle is a traditional sweetener for many cakes, but the modern equivalent, golden syrup, is much sweeter and does not affect the colour of the cake. Honey is used in a few cakes but can cause considerable darkening during cooking. If it is to be substituted for sugar in a standard recipe, only one-third of the total should be honey.

Fat may be varied according to the budget, but each fat has a characteristic flavour which will yield a different end-product. Butter has a beautiful flavour but produces a slightly heavier cake, and is not quite so easy to cream. Block margarine may be used for rubbed-in cakes, and gives a good result in well-spiced or heavily fruited cakes, where the lack of butter flavour will not be noticed. Soft margarine is very easy to use for creamed mixtures and gives a soft light texture, and the flavour is masked by chocolate, coffee, etc. Many old-fashioned cakes were made with dripping from the large pieces of meat which were frequently cooked. The fat was collected in bowls, and would be clarified for the best results, but today it is only occasionally mentioned in farmhouse fruit cake recipes. Lard was also widely used as it was so easily made from the cottage pig, and was a very clean fat. It is particularly good for the rubbed-in mixtures cooked on a griddle, or may be mixed with other fats. It gives a flaky texture to pastry.

Eggs are sold in a wide range of sizes. Unless otherwise stated, use a No 3 egg which is medium sized. If you are uncertain of the size, use an egg which weighs 2 oz (50 g). Eggs should be used at room temperature. They give volume, colour and flavour to cakes, but are occasionally replaced in old-fashioned recipes by vinegar, which reacts with milk and a raising agent to give a light cake, but no detectable flavour.

Dried fruit should be fresh, clean and plump. Usually packaged fruit is very clean, but it is always worth examining as pieces of stem or pips are sometimes undetected at the factory. Peel may be bought in the piece or ready chopped. The former generally has a better flavour but may be rather hard. Glacé cherries are usually very syrupy and sticky and should be washed, then drained and dried before use or they may sink in a cake.

Flavourings should be as pure as possible. It is always best to use brandy, rum or sherry instead of equivalent flavouring. Plain chocolate and cocoa give a stronger, clearer flavour than milk chocolate in baking, and both are preferable to the modern 'flavoured cooking chocolate' which is cheaper, but very fatty and with a poor flavour. Vanilla flavour may be introduced by a vanilla pod which has been buried in caster sugar which takes on the pure scent of the vanilla beans. Flavoured oils such as lemon or peppermint are pure and strong, and give a far better flavour than the equivalent essences, but they must be used very sparingly. Coffee essence has an excellent flavour but is very sweet, so many people prefer to reduce fresh strong coffee until it is very syrupy, or to use strong instant coffee dissolved in a little hot water. Ground spices should always be very fresh, and should only be bought in very small quantities as they go stale quickly.

Equipment

For centuries cakes have been beaten with the bare hands, or with a bowl and wooden spoon, so today's mixers and processors are not strictly necessary in this branch of cooking. However, they do produce beautifully light and well-mixed cakes and save considerable time, although the cook must beware of over-beating which produces a heavy cake. A hand rotary beater, or hand-held electric mixer will produce very good results, while a wire balloon whisk is excellent for whisking eggs as it helps to incorporate a lot of air.

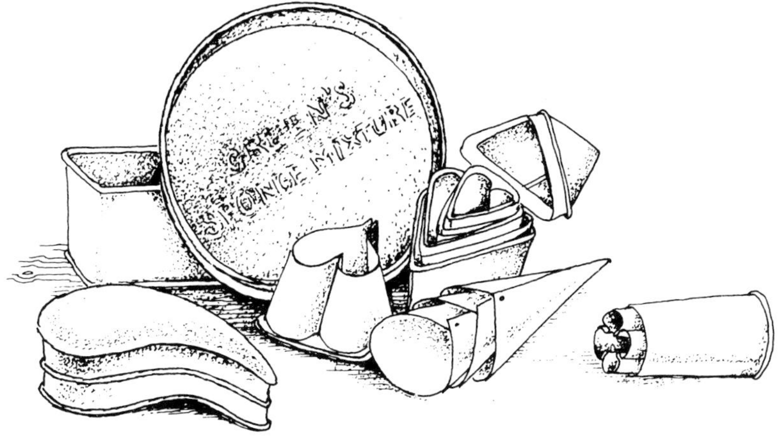

Tins are necessary to shape most cakes, but if you are an inexperienced baker do not be tempted to buy a wide range of shapes and sizes. A pair of 7 in. (17.5 cm) sponge sandwich tins is very useful, together with a 7 in. (17.5 cm) and an 8 in. (20 cm) round cake tin which should be about 3 in. (7.5 cm) deep. If these tins have removable bases, they will be easier to use. For some fruit cakes, and for gingerbreads, square or rectangular tins will be necessary, about 2 in. (5 cm) deep. A 7 in. (17.5 cm)square tin is useful, and a larger one about 7 × 11 in. (17.5 × 27.5 cm). Often a meat roasting tin may be used for these cakes and will save extra equipment. Shallow rectangular tins are for biscuits, scones and Swiss rolls and usually two tins will be needed. A sheet of tartlet tins is useful for pastry items and small cakes, and may also be used for individual savoury items such as cheese tarts (look for a tin with 12 or 18 indentations). 1 lb (450 g) and 2 lb (900 g) loaf tins are often used and may also be used for meat loaves, patés and puddings, so are not an unnecessary expense.

A wire rack is important for cooling cakes, so that air circulates and the warm air is dispersed and prevents the cake from becoming heavy. In emergency, the rack of a grill pan may be used.

Storage tins or airtight plastic boxes are necessary for storage. Separate containers should be kept for cakes and biscuits, as cakes will make biscuits soft if stored together.

Paper of various types plays an important part in the successful preparation of cakes. Greaseproof paper is used for lining tins, but non-stick baking parchment is ideal for tins on which slightly sticky mixtures such as brandy snaps or meringues are cooked. Rice paper is used for one or two special cakes such as macaroons, and is edible. Small paper cases may be used for individual cakes.

Methods and cake-making terms

There are some specific terms used for the processes involved, and it is helpful to know what methods they refer to.

Rubbing-in is used for plain cakes, biscuits and pastry. The fat should be cut into small pieces and rubbed very lightly into the flour with the fingertips until the mixture is like fine breadcrumbs.

Creaming is used for a variety of cakes and involves beating sugar and fat at room temperature until the mixture is soft, fluffy and pale. The fat must not be melted or it will be difficult to incorporate air.

Whisking is for very light cakes in which whole eggs, or separated whites, are whipped with sugar until very light and fluffy. When whole eggs are used the mixture will look like lightly whipped cream; with egg whites the mixture will form soft peaks (for incorporating into heavier mixtures) or stiff peaks for some small cakes which need to keep their shape. Egg whites must be whisked in a fat-free bowl with a scrupulously clean whisk or they will not whisk up successfully.

Beating is specified for some cakes, usually when a melted or liquid mixture has to be added to dry ingredients, and this may be done with a wooden spoon, or a mixer. Rich fruit cakes and sponge cakes should not be beaten or their texture will be spoiled.

Folding-in is a method used to incorporate ingredients very gently so that air is not driven out of a mixture. Light mixtures such as whisked egg whites are folded into heavier ones, and flour is folded into creamed mixtures. This should be done with a knife or metal spoon, using a sharp cutting action, and using the knife or spoon in a figure-of-eight shape, lifting the heavier mixture from the bottom of the bowl. The mixture should not be overworked or patted flat, and the folding-in operation should be finished as soon as the two mixtures have been incorporated.

Melting is necessary for most gingerbreads and is also used for boiled fruit cakes. The fat and syrup or treacle are heated together until the fat has melted and the treacle is thin and runny, so that the mixture can easily be mixed into the dry ingredients. Sometimes the sugar and fruit in a recipe are also heated in the same pan, so that the sugar dissolves and the fruit becomes plump.

Consistency is the name for the texture and weight of the cake mixture before baking. *Soft dropping consistency* means that the mixture will drop easily from a spoon or whisk when shaken, but it will be too stiff to pour. *Stiff dropping consistency* indicates that the mixture will keep its shape when shaken from a spoon, but is still too soft and sticky to handle. *Soft dough* means that the mixture is soft and light and can be rolled out.

Baking

It is very important to use the tin size specified in a recipe, or the volume of the cake, and its consequent cooking time, will be altered and the cake will be ruined. The correct temperature must also be used, and the oven should be preheated for about 10 minutes before use (this timing varies a great deal). If you are unsuccessful with the temperature specified in this book, it may well be that your oven is unreliable and should be checked with an oven thermometer or by the supplier, as there may often be a difference of 25°F or more between the indicated and actual temperatures.

In general, cakes with a high sugar content, such as gingerbread and rich fruit cakes, are baked at a lower temperature; sponge cakes at a moderate temperature and scones and yeast mixtures at a high temperature. Cakes should be baked in the centre of the oven unless otherwise specified.

A cooked cake will be well-risen and golden, firm but not crusty and slightly springy when pressed lightly, and will shrink slightly away from the edges of the tin. An old-fashioned test is to listen for a cake 'singing' as it is withdrawn from the oven. If there is a slight noise from the cake leave it to cook a little longer. The final test is to insert a thin skewer or knife in the centre of the cake, which should come out cleanly without any uncooked mixture clinging to it.

Sponge cakes may be turned out of their tins as soon as cooked, but more solid mixtures such as fruit cakes and gingerbreads are best left for 10–15 minutes before turning out so that they firm up. Cooling should be completed on a wire rack, and biscuits which appear to be soft when lifted from a baking tray will become crisp on the rack. Cool cakes completely before storing in a tin or freezer.

Quantities

An 8 in. (20 cm) spongecake will cut into approximately 8 slices; a fruit cake of the same size will yield 12 slices as the cake is more filling. When planning a party, allow for the fact that people may want to try a number of different cakes, so smaller slices may be permissible. Allow 2 small items and 2 slices from larger cakes for each person. If you want to prepare a double or treble quantity of cake mixture, this is perfectly possible, although the total quantity may be difficult to handle. It is most important, however, that the mixture should be baked in the specified tins e.g. make three 8 in. (20 cm) cakes, rather than one or two larger ones as cooking time is greatly affected by the volume of the raw mixture.

Storage

A rich fruit cake (e.g. Celebration Cake p. 77) will keep for up to a year in an airtight tin or plastic storage container. Plainer cakes are best stored no longer than two weeks in the same type of container. Biscuits will also keep well for 2–3 weeks, as will unfilled meringues. Fatless spongecakes and iced cakes are not suitable for storage by this method, and fatless spongecakes should be eaten while very fresh.

Sponge sandwiches made with fat and butter-iced cakes may be frozen for up to 4 months, as may yeast buns and cakes. There is no point in wasting freezer space on other types of cakes.

3 *Griddlecakes, Scones and Potato Cakes*

I took him in and gied him a scone.
(Scottish song)

The earliest form of home-baking was on the bakestone set in a hot fire on the down-hearth at the side of the room. Only large houses or professional bakeries could boast an oven, although some farmhouses had a small beehive-shaped bread oven set in the wall. These ovens were difficult to regulate, and most people took bread to the communal village oven for baking and finishing. In remote areas this was not possible, and some other method of baking had to be devised. In the West Country there were free-standing clay ovens which could be placed in the fire, and some people used iron cauldrons, with a lid which could be closely covered by hot coals or peat so that the all-round heat could be used to bake primitive bread. The country wife, however, found it easiest to spread her dough or batter on the hot bakestone which would seal and cook one side; the circle of dough could then be turned so that it finished cooking on the other side.

From the bakestone, the griddle or girdle developed, which was a thick flat iron plate on a very long handle or on a loop so that it could be suspended over the flames. This method of preparing breads and sweet breads remained extremely popular in the more remote areas of the British Isles, so that griddlecakes and scones are still the pride of the Scots, Welsh and Irish kitchen.

These flat cakes did not contain yeast and were quickly made, so that they were very useful emergency treats for the family, as they consisted of little more than richly fatted flour, sometimes enlivened by spice, sugar, fresh fruit or dried fruit. The potato was often used with a little flour to give a moist cake, and this was very economical whether served plain, or with dried fruit, or being mixed with apples. Floury potatoes give the best result and should be boiled in their skins. When they are just cooked the water should be drained away and the potatoes covered with a folded teacloth and lid for a few minutes so that they become delightfully floury and light. They should then be peeled while still warm, cooled and mashed or grated before mixing with the other ingredients.

It is not difficult to use a griddle on top of today's stoves, but a heavy frying pan may be used instead. The griddle should be heated while the dough or batter is being prepared, but it must not be too hot. As a test sprinkle on a little flour, and if it browns at once the griddle is too hot. When the flour takes some time to colour gradually, the griddle is at the correct temperature. When using a griddle it should be floured for a dough, but greased for batter. The griddle should only be lightly greased with a piece of suet or a brushing of lard, and should never be washed but only rubbed when hot with a little salt and then wiped with a clean paper or piece of cloth.

Griddle recipes may be adapted for the oven, with the cakes or scones placed on a baking sheet. This may be lightly greased, but for a traditional floury base sprinkle a little flour on the baking sheet before putting on the cakes. These cakes are best prepared in a hot oven (425–450°F/220–230°C/Gas Mark 7–8) according to the recipe.

Potato Scones

8 oz (225 g) potatoes
2 oz (50 g) butter
4 oz (100 g) plain flour
½ tsp baking powder
¼ tsp salt

Peel the potatoes and boil them until tender. Drain well and mash with butter. Sieve together flour, baking powder and salt and add to the potatoes. Knead well to make a pliable dough. Roll out ½ in. (1.25 cm) thick on a lightly floured board. Cut into rounds and prick with a fork. Cook on a hot dry griddle (or thick frying pan) for 4 minutes on each side. If preferred, bake at 425°F/220°C/Gas Mark 7 for 10 minutes. Serve hot with butter.

Irish Potato Apple Cakes

4 large potatoes
2 oz (50 g) melted butter
2 oz (50 g) plain flour
½ tsp baking powder
¼ tsp salt
8 oz (225 g) eating apples
1½ oz (40 g) butter
1 oz (25 g) sugar
½ tsp ground cinnamon

Preheat oven to 400°F/200°C/Gas Mark 6. Peel the potatoes and boil them until tender. Drain well and mash with melted butter. Sieve together flour, baking powder and salt and add to the potatoes. Knead well to make a pliable dough. Divide into two pieces and roll into rounds about ½ in. (1.25 cm) thick. Divide each round into four triangles. Peel and slice the apples and arrange on four triangles. Cover with remaining triangles, pressing the edges together lightly. Place on a lightly greased baking sheet and bake for 25 minutes until golden brown. Carefully lift the top of each triangle and cover the apples with flakes of butter and a sprinkling of sugar and cinnamon. Replace the tops and return to the oven for 3 minutes. Serve at once.

Pratie Oaten

This is another of the good potato cakes for which Ireland is famous, deriving its name from 'pratie' – slang for 'potato'.

1 lb (450 g) cooked mashed potatoes
8 oz (225 g) fine oatmeal
Salt and pepper
¼ pt (150 ml) milk

Put the potatoes, oatmeal, salt and pepper into a bowl and mix thoroughly. Add enough milk to give a dough which can be rolled out. Dust a pastry board lightly with oatmeal and roll out the dough about 1 in. (2.5 cm) thick. Cut into small triangles or circles with a scone cutter. Cook on an ungreased griddle for about 5 minutes each side until golden. Serve hot with butter.

Plain Girdle Scones

8 oz (225 g) self-raising flour
¼ tsp salt
1½ oz (40 g) butter
1 oz (25 g) granulated sugar
¼ pt (150 ml) milk

Sieve the flour and salt into a bowl. Rub in the butter until the mixture is like fine crumbs. Stir in the sugar and mix with the milk to make a firm but soft dough. Knead well and roll the dough ½ in. (1.25 cm) thick. Cut into 2 in. (5 cm) rounds. Cook on a hot floured griddle until the undersides are golden brown. Turn carefully and continue cooking until the sides are golden brown and the scones are cooked through.

Scones

These plain cake/breads are great favourites for teatime and very quickly made. The basic mixture may be varied so that the scones are savoury or sweet, but the basic method remains the same. It is important that the fat is rubbed in very lightly so that plenty of air is incorporated into the mixture. Sour milk makes particularly light and delicious scones. Plain scones are at their best served with strawberry jam and thick cream.

8 oz (225 g) plain flour
½ tsp bicarbonate of soda
½ tsp cream of tartar
2 oz (50 g) butter
1 oz (25 g) sugar
6–7 tbsp sour milk

Flour a baking sheet lightly. Preheat oven to 450°F/230°C/Gas Mark 8.

Sift the flour with the bicarbonate of soda and cream of tartar. Rub in the butter very lightly until the mixture is like fine breadcrumbs. Stir in the sugar and add enough milk to give a soft light dough which can be rolled easily. Roll out on a lightly floured board to ½ in. (1.25 cm) thick. Cut into 2 in. (5 cm) rounds with a plain cutter. Put the scones on to the baking sheet so that they just touch each other (this will make sure the sides are soft when the scones are cooked). Brush the tops with a little milk and bake for 12 minutes. Lift on to a wire rack to cool. Serve freshly cooked, either split and buttered, or with jam and cream.

Cheese Scones

Omit sugar and add 3 oz (75 g) grated Cheddar cheese and a pinch of pepper and mustard powder.

Fruit Scones

Add 3 oz (75 g) mixed dried fruit to basic scone mixture.

Oaten Tea Scones

12 oz (50 g) medium oatmeal
4 oz (100 g) plain flour
1 tsp bicarbonate of soda
1 tsp cream of tartar
¼ tsp salt
2 oz (50 g) sugar
4 oz (100 g) butter *or* margarine
¼ pt (150 ml) sour milk

Preheat oven to 400°F/200°C/Gas Mark 6. Flour a baking sheet. Stir together oatmeal, flour, soda, cream of tartar, salt and sugar. Rub in the butter or margarine until the mixture is like fine breadcrumbs. Add the milk to make a firm, soft, dough (more milk may be needed, but the dough should be firm enough to roll). Roll out ½ in. (1.25 cm) thick and cut into 2 in. (5 cm) rounds. Place on the baking sheet and bake for 20 minutes.

Treacle Scones

These dark spiced scones are a speciality of Scotland and should be served split and buttered while very fresh.

8 oz (225 g) self-raising flour
Pinch of salt
½ tsp bicarbonate of soda
1 tsp ground mixed spice
½ oz (15 g) dark soft brown sugar
1 oz (25 g) butter
2 tbsp black treacle
¼ pt (150 ml) milk

Flour a baking sheet lightly. Preheat oven to 425°F/220°C/Gas Mark 7. Sift together the flour, salt, soda and spice and stir in the sugar. Rub in the butter until the mixture is like coarse breadcrumbs. Mix with the treacle and milk to give a soft dough. Roll out on a floured board ½ in. (1.25 cm) thick. Cut into 2 in. (5 cm) rounds with a plain cutter. Flour the baking sheet lightly. Put on the scones so that they just touch each other. Bake for 15 minutes. Cool on a wire rack, split and butter.

Drop Scones

8 oz (225 g) self-raising flour
2 oz (50 g) caster sugar
2 eggs
½ pt (300 ml) milk
1 tsp cream of tartar

Sieve the flour into a bowl and stir in the sugar. Add the eggs and milk with the cream of tartar, beating well to make a thick batter. Grease a griddle or thick frying pan lightly and warm to moderate heat. Pour on tablespoonsful of batter and cook over moderate heat until bubbles form on the surface of the scones and burst. Turn carefully with a palette knife and cook the other side until golden. Wrap warm scones in a clean cloth to keep them soft, and eat freshly made.

Singin' Hinny

The cake takes its name from the singing noise made as it cooks and 'hinny' is a term of endearment in Northumberland.

8 oz (225 g) plain flour
½ tsp baking powder
½ tsp salt
2 oz (50 g) butter
2 oz (50 g) lard
3 oz (75 g) currants
¼ pt (150 ml) milk

Grease a griddle or thick frying pan lightly. Sift the flour, baking powder and salt. Rub in the butter and lard until the mixture is like fine breadcrumbs. Add the currants and enough milk to make a stiff dough. Roll out to one large round about 1 in. (2.5 cm) thick. Prick lightly all over with a fork. Heat the griddle or frying pan. Put on the cake and cook until lightly golden on the base. Turn carefully and cook the other side until golden. Turn back to the first side and cook 1 minute longer. Lift off the griddle or frying pan and split horizontally while hot. Spread with butter and serve at once.

Sussex Plum Heavies

These little scones are very far from being 'heavy' but there is a story that they are really 'heva cakes' and the name derives from the call made to encourage those who pull the fishing boats up the Sussex shores.

8 oz (225 g) self-raising flour
Pinch of salt
2 oz (50 g) butter
1 tbsp caster sugar
3 oz (75 g) currants and sultanas
1 egg
5 tbsp sour milk
Additional caster sugar for sprinkling

Grease a baking sheet. Preheat oven to 450°F/230°C/Gas Mark 8. Sieve the flour and salt together. Rub in the butter until the mixture is like fine breadcrumbs. Stir in the sugar and dried fruit. Beat the egg and milk together and add most of the liquid to the dried ingredients. Mix to a soft dough. Roll out 1 in. (2.5 cm) thick and cut into 2 in. (5 cm) squares. Brush with remaining egg-and-milk and sprinkle lightly with caster sugar. Bake for 15 minutes. Cool on a wire rack.

Oatcakes

Oats grow better than any other cereal in Scotland, and oatmeal formed part of the staple diet. Oatcakes were eaten with nearly every meal, and they are extremely good with cheese or with marmalade. They may be eaten when freshly made, but are improved by being left in a cool oven until crisp.

4 oz (100 g) medium oatmeal
1 oz (25 g) plain flour
1 oz (25 g) butter
1 oz (25 g) lard
½ oz (15 g) sugar
Pinch of salt
Pinch of soda
2–3 tbsp boiling water

Preheat oven to 450°F/230°C/Gas Mark 8. Stir together the oatmeal and flour. Cut the butter and lard into small pieces and stir into the mixture. Sprinkle on sugar, salt and soda. Add boiling water and knead the mixture until firm but pliable. Sprinkle oatmeal on a board and roll one-quarter of the mixture into a thin round. Divide into 4 triangles and place on a lightly greased baking sheet. Repeat with each quarter of the dough. Bake for 7 minutes. Turn over oatcakes and continue baking for 3 minutes. Place a cooling rack in a roasting tin and arrange the oatcakes on this. Leave in a plate warming oven for 5–6 hours until the oatcakes are crisp. If preferred, the oatcakes may be cooked on a floured griddle before drying.

Dorset Apple Cake

This is yet another country cake which would originally have been prepared on a griddle, but is now more easily baked in the oven.

8 oz (225 g) plain flour
1½ tsp baking powder
Pinch of salt
4 oz (100 g) lard *or* butter
8 oz (225 g) eating apples
4 oz (100 g) sugar
1 egg

Grease an 8 in. (20 cm) round cake tin. Preheat oven to 350°F/180°C/Gas Mark 4. Sieve the flour, baking powder and salt together and rub in the fat until the mixture is like fine breadcrumbs. Peel and core the apples and chop them roughly. Stir into the mixture with the sugar and mix to a dough with the egg. Spread the mixture about 1 in. (2.5 cm) thick in the prepared tin. Bake for 50 minutes. Lift on to a wire rack to cool slightly. While still warm, split in half and spread with butter before replacing the top. If liked, a few currants or sultanas may be added.

Fat Rascals

These little cakes from Yorkshire are rather like rich fruit scones with a childishly comforting name like the Singin' Hinny of Northumberland (p. 26). They are also known as Turf Cakes, as they used to be cooked on the moors in the open air with the aid of a griddle over a turf fire.

4 oz (100 g) lard or butter
8 oz (225 g) self-raising flour
Pinch of salt
3 oz (75 g) sugar
2 oz (50 g) currants
2 oz (50 g) sultanas
2 tbsp milk
1 tbsp water
Caster sugar for sprinkling

Grease two baking sheets. Preheat oven to 425°F/220°C/Gas Mark 7. Rub the lard or butter into the flour until the mixture is like fine breadcrumbs. Add the salt, sugar, currants and sultanas. Mix to a soft dough with the milk and water. Roll out ½ in. (1.25 cm) thick. Cut out rounds with the rim of a tumbler. Put on greased baking sheets and sprinkle with sugar. Bake for 15 minutes. Cool on a wire rack.

Cornish Tettie Cake

A lump of butcher's suet is best to use for this as the flakes of grated suet make the mixture light and rich. If fresh suet is unobtainable, packet suet, butter or margarine may be used instead. Mrs Rowse, an old lady who gave me this recipe, remembered her mother rolling the 'cake' out to fit a big metal sheath, or baking sheet, which fitted into her blackleaded range.

1½ lb (675 g) mashed potatoes
Salt and pepper
8 oz (225 g) plain flour
8 oz (225 g) suet

Lightly flour a baking sheet. Preheat oven to 400°F/200°C/Gas Mark 6. The potatoes may be used hot or cold and should be seasoned to taste. Sieve the flour and beat into the potatoes. Grate the suet or chop it very finely, and stir into the potatoes (if using butter or margarine, soften the fat without melting, and stir into the potatoes). Squeeze the mixture together to form a ball. Place on the baking sheet and pat into a circle or rectangle about 1 in. (2.5 cm) thick. Use a sharp knife to score the top to make a criss-cross pattern. Bake for 45 minutes until golden. Serve hot with butter.

Teisen Lap

Traditionally this cake was baked in a Dutch oven in front of an open fire, but now it cooks in the oven, or may be baked on a griddle. The cake should only be about 1 in. (2.5 cm) thick, and for the finest results should be made with sour milk or buttermilk.

8 oz (225 g) plain flour
1 tsp baking powder
Pinch of salt
Pinch of ground nutmeg
2 oz (50 g) butter
2 oz (50 g) sugar
2 oz (50 g) mixed currants and sultanas
2 eggs
¼ pt (150 ml) milk

Grease a 7 × 11 in. (17.5 × 27.5 cm) rectangular tin. Preheat oven to 350°F/180°C/Gas Mark 4. Sieve the flour, baking powder, salt and nutmeg. Rub in the butter until the mixture is like fine breadcrumbs. Stir in the sugar and dried fruit. Beat the eggs and milk together and add to the dry ingredients, making a soft dough. Spread in the tin. Bake for 40 minutes. Cut in squares and serve freshly baked. Alternatively, roll out the dough 1 in. (2.5 cm) thick and bake on a floured griddle or frying pan for 15 minutes on each side until golden.

Welsh Cakes

8 oz (225 g) self-raising flour
Pinch of salt
2 oz (50 g) butter
2 oz (50 g) lard
3 oz (75 g) caster sugar
2 oz (50 g) currants
1 tbsp grated lemon rind
1 egg
¼ pt (150 ml) milk

Sieve the flour and salt into a bowl. Rub in the butter and lard until the mixture looks like fine breadcrumbs. Stir in the sugar, currants and lemon rind. Beat the egg and milk together and add to the dry ingredients, making a soft dough. Roll out lightly to about ¼ in. (65 mm) thick and cut into 2 in. rounds. Bake on floured griddle or frying pan until golden on both sides. Sprinkle with a little extra caster sugar and serve freshly baked.

Highland Slim Cakes

These quickly made thin cakes were traditionally eaten for breakfast or tea, and had to be eaten up at one meal as they become tough if kept. They should be served hot, fresh from the griddle.

1 lb (450 g) plain flour
4 oz (100 g) butter
½ pt (300 ml) milk
2 eggs

Sieve the flour into a bowl and rub in the butter until the mixture is like fine breadcrumbs. Heat the milk to lukewarm and add to the flour. Beat well, adding the eggs. Work quickly and roll out the dough lightly about ½ in. (1.25 cm) thick. Cut out with the top of a bowl, saucer or drinking glass. Bake on a lightly floured griddle or frying pan until golden on both sides.

Cornish Heavy Cake

Like Sussex Plum Heavies (p. 27), this cake is certainly not 'heavy'. The cake was originally called Heva Cake after the shout 'Heva' given to the pilchard fishermen to tell them that their nets were full and ready to pull in. The shout was given by a man called the Huer, who lived in a hut on the cliffs near Newquay (a popular holiday keepsake used to be a china model of the hut made by W. Goss Ltd) and after the fish were safely gathered, the men would return to their 'heva' cake for tea. Originally the cake would have been prepared on a bakestone or griddle, but it is now more easily baked in the oven.

1 lb (450 g) plain flour
¼ tsp salt
½ tsp ground mixed spice
4 oz (100 g) lard
4 oz (100 g) mixed dried fruit
2 oz (50 g) chopped mixed candied peel
3 oz (75 g) sugar
½ pt (300 ml) milk
4 oz (100 g) butter
Beaten egg for glazing

Grease a baking sheet. Preheat oven to 400°F/200°C/Gas Mark 6. Sieve the flour, salt and spice into a bowl. Cut the lard into small pieces and rub into the flour until the mixture is like fine breadcrumbs. Stir in the dried fruit, peel and sugar. Add enough milk to make a soft dough. Roll out into an oblong about 16 × 18 in. (40 × 45 cm) and mark lightly into thirds. Dot half the butter over the top two-thirds of the dough, fold over bottom third and top with the remainder. Give the dough a halfturn, roll out and repeat the process. Roll out about 7 × 10 in. (17.5 × 25 cm) and 1 in. (2.5 cm) thick. Place on baking tray and score with a knife in diamond shapes. Brush with beaten egg to glaze. Bake for 30 minutes. Eat warm.

Hunmanby Cream Cake

This is another of the quickly made farmhouse cakes which was probably originally prepared on a griddle, but now is more easily baked in the oven. The cream would have been thick and rich, but now 'double' cream will have to do. The original recipe was made with the aid of a large breakfast cup, but I have translated the measurements for modern use.

2 eggs
¼ pt (150 ml) double cream
8 oz (225 g) granulated sugar
6 oz (150 g) plain flour
2 tsp baking powder

Grease a 7 in. (17.5 cm) round cake tin. Preheat oven to 425°F/220°C/ Gas Mark 7. Beat the eggs and cream together and then beat in the sugar until the mixture is very thick and creamy. Gradually beat in the sieved flour and baking powder. Pour into the tin. Bake for 20 minutes. Serve hot.

Welsh Bakestone Tart

This double-crust fruit tart was originally cooked on a greased bakestone or griddle and turned half-way through cooking. It may be prepared in a thick frying pan, but is now most easily baked in the oven. Although traditionally made with blackberries, it may also be prepared with rhubarb, gooseberries or apples. Additional sugar will probably be required after baking.

8 oz (225 g) shortcrust pastry
12 oz (350 g) blackberries
1 oz (25 g) butter
3 oz (75 g) light soft brown sugar

Grease a baking sheet. Preheat oven to 400°F/200°C/Gas Mark 6. Roll out the pastry into a circle and put the fruit on half of it. Fold over the edges and seal them firmly. Bake for 20 minutes, then reduce heat to 350°F/ 180°C/Gas Mark 4 and continue baking for 25 minutes. Lift on to a serving dish and gently lift the top. Insert small pieces of butter and sprinkle in the sugar. Serve freshly baked.

Bakestone Fruit Scones

These little drop scones filled with fresh fruit were originally made in Wales on a bakestone, but today we may use a griddle or heavy frying pan. Tiny wild strawberries, blackberries, wild raspberries or the garden varieties may be added to the batter.

4 oz (100 g) self-raising flour
Pinch of salt
½ tsp baking powder
1 egg
½ pt (300 ml) sour milk
4 oz (100 g) fresh berries

Sift together the flour, salt and baking powder. Add the egg and enough milk to make a thick creamy batter. Drop tablespoonsful of the mixture on to a hot greased griddle and sprinkle each scone with fruit. Cook until the base of each scone is golden, then turn and cook the other side until set and golden. Sprinkle with sugar and serve hot.

4 *Yeastcakes and Buns*

Now for the banquet we press;
Now for the eggs and the ham!
Now for the mustard and cress!
Now for the strawberry jam!
Now for the tea of our host!
Now for the rollicking bun!
Now for the muffin and toast!
Now for the gay Sally Lunn.

(W. S. Gilbert, *Bab Ballads*)

The gloriously fruited yeast cake was well described by Flora Thompson in *Lark Rise to Candleford* under the name of 'baker's cake'. It was

> a rich, fruit, spicy dough cake, obtained in the following manner. The housewife provided all the ingredients excepting the dough, putting raisins and currants, lard, sugar and spice in a basin which she gave to the baker, who added the dough, made and baked the cake, and returned it, beautifully browned in his big oven. The charge was the same as that for a loaf of bread the same size, and the result was delicious.

For generations an enriched bread had been the basic cake of most families, often consisting of layers of bread dough with lard to give a soft flaky loaf. Sweet mixtures, such as lardy cake, added dried fruit and sugar to the lard, producing a very rich and fattening mixture which is highly addictive. When every cottager kept a pig, lard was the most commonly used fat and invaluable for producing these treats from ordinary bread dough.

Other treats were the sweetened breads which included the spices and dried fruit in the dough, and small individual buns were particularly popular for festive occasions. These were also easy to make in Tudor times when they first became popular, for they were simply made from the household dough with the sweet ingredients kneaded in. Since these were festive buns with religious significance, bakers were forbidden by an order of 1592 to prepare them except for funerals, Good Friday and Christmas. If the spiced bread, buns or biscuits were prepared against the law, they had to be given to the poor, which may be the origin of so many local customs of bun-distribution for the poor of the parish.

These special buns had to be prepared at home if at all, but by the time of James I it became difficult to enforce such laws, and the delicious buns were again prepared professionally, except for an eclipse under the Puritans who thought such things were popish. The bun reached its greatest favour in Georgian times when bun houses became popular in London and in fashionable spa towns, where the sweet breads were eaten as snacks with chocolate, coffee or tea. There are hundreds of local bun specialities, some flavoured with saffron, or caraway, or topped with sugar crystals. Only the Hot Cross Bun is still marked with the pagan crooked cross of Astarte, as all baked goods used to be to ward off evil spirits.

The original yeast was barm or ale yeast, which was liquid and strongly flavoured, often bitter. From the quantities used, it would seem that the liquid weakened the yeast and its rising qualities, and housewives did not appreciate the flavour of this brewer's yeast. Hannah Glasse, Eliza Acton and many other cookery writers recommended washing the yeast and leaving it overnight in fresh water before use. Eliza Acton also recommended mixing the yeast with a little brown sugar to strengthen it and improve the ferment.

The more convenient compressed German yeast began to be used in England in the middle of the nineteenth century which greatly speeded up the process of baking, and gave a fresher, lighter and pleasanter-tasting bread. Some bakers and housewives followed very old methods and prepared their own yeast from fermented cereals, boiled potatoes or flour, or used Parisian barm made from flour and salt.

Compressed yeast with its putty-like colour and texture is still widely used when it can be obtained from bakers or health food shops. Dried yeast is most widely available in packets or cans and is easy to use if fresh, but it deteriorates rapidly once exposed to air, and then refuses to ferment. The newest yeast of all is 'fermipan' which does not have to be reconstituted with sugar or liquid but is mixed directly into the dry ingredients before any liquid is added. It is very important to check which type of yeast is being used before starting on a fermented dough recipe. If using fresh or dried yeast, the yeast must be seen to be working vigorously before being added to the dry ingredients. Gentle warmth encourages yeast to develop, as does the addition of a little sugar (doughs may be refrigerated or left in a cold place overnight, but must be returned to a warm temperature before they start working again).

Bath Buns

Bath was a fashionable spa during the eighteenth and early nineteenth centuries, where Society went to see and be seen, to take the waters and to attend parties, concerts and balls. The city also seemed to be a gathering place for good bakers whose specialities such as Sally Lunns and Bath Oliver biscuits are still part of our culinary vocabulary. The fashionable Georgian bun made in Bath was a slightly flat and bumpy cake topped with a sticky glaze and a sprinkling of crushed sugar. They were originally flavoured with caraway, and sugared caraway comfits were sometimes used on the top instead of the sugar. This roughly crushed sugar was derived from the sugar loaf, weighing 14 lb (6.5 kg) and shaped like a steeple hat, which was the only form of sugar available during the eighteenth and much of the nineteenth century. These loaves were wrapped in blue paper and suspended from the ceiling of bakers, shops and private kitchens. Huge sugar nippers like garden shears were used to break the sugar into manageable pieces, which were further reduced to small lumps with more delicate cutters. Today we must crush sugar cubes to get the right topping for these buns which have retained their popularity for centuries. Until the 1950s they were a speciality of the Paddington Station tearoom and of Lyons Corner Houses.

12 oz (350 g) bread flour
Pinch of salt
4 oz (100 g) butter
2½ fl oz (65 ml) milk
½ oz (15 g) fresh yeast *or* ¼ oz (7 g) dried yeast
2 eggs
1 tsp sugar
3 oz (75 g) sugar
Grated rind of 1 lemon
3 oz (75 g) sultanas
1 oz (25 g) chopped mixed candied peel
Beaten egg to glaze
Cube sugar

Grease a baking sheet. Sieve the flour and salt into a warm bowl. Rub in the butter until the mixture is like fine breadcrumbs. Warm the milk and mix in the yeast and leave until the yeast is frothing. Add to the dry ingredients with the eggs and mix to a soft dough. Cover and leave in a warm place for 45 minutes. Knead in the sugar, lemon rind, sultanas and peel and form into 10 rough balls. Put on to the baking sheet and flatten slightly with the hand. Leave in a warm place for 10 minutes. Meanwhile, preheat oven to 450°F/230°C/Gas Mark 8. Brush the buns with beaten egg and sprinkle with roughly crushed cube sugar. Bake for 15 minutes. Cool on a wire rack.

Chelsea Buns

These square buns which are wrapped round the spiced fruit filling originated at the Chelsea Bun House in Pimlico Road, London, which the Hand family ran in the eighteenth century. Mr Richard Hand was a flamboyant dresser, known as Captain Bun, and even royalty patronised his fashionable eating house. A very rich version of the bun is found in America under the name of a Philadelphia Sticky Bun, so possibly this delectable Chelsea confection was exported with a Georgian settler.

Dough
12 oz (350 g) bread flour
3 oz (75 g) butter
⅓ pt (200 ml) milk
½ oz (15 g) fresh yeast *or* ¼ oz (7 g) dried yeast
1½ oz (40 g) currants
1½ oz (40 g) sugar
Beaten egg

Glaze
1 tsp granulated sugar
2 tbsp milk
Caster sugar for sprinkling

Grease a 10 × 14 in. (25 × 35 cm) roasting tin or cake tin with deep sides. Sieve the flour into a warm bowl. Rub in 2 oz (50 g) butter. Warm the milk and mix a little with the yeast, then add the remaining milk and leave until the yeast is frothing. Add to the flour, mix well and knead to a smooth dough. Cover and leave in a warm place for 45 minutes. Knead again and roll lightly into a rectangle. Melt the remaining butter and brush over the surface of the dough. Sprinkle with currants and sugar and roll up like a Swiss Roll. Cut across in 1½ in. (3.75 cm) slices. Put cut side up in the tin about ½ in. (1.25 cm) apart. Leave in a warm place for 10 minutes and brush with a little beaten egg. Meanwhile preheat oven to 450°F/230°C/Gas Mark 8. Bake for 15 minutes. For the glaze melt the sugar in the milk and brush over the buns as they come from the oven, then sprinkle lightly with caster sugar. Leave in the tin until cool.

Revel Buns

Village festivities in the West Country were known as 'revels', and there are many foods associated with such occasions, such as syllabub and junket. These buns were traditionally baked in sycamore leaves, but sometimes the mixture was simply baked as loaves. Like so many West Country dishes these buns were lightly coloured with saffron, and included rich cream as part of the fat content.

1 lb (450 g) bread flour
1 tsp salt
2 oz (50 g) lard
¼ pt (150 ml) thick cream

Pinch of ground cinnamon
Pinch of saffron
3 tbsp milk
½ oz (15 g) fresh yeast *or* ¼ oz (7 g) dried yeast
1 egg
6 oz (150 g) currants
Icing sugar for sprinkling

If possible, flavour and colour the milk the day before. To do this, dissolve the saffron in the milk and leave to stand overnight. Sieve the flour, salt and cinnamon into a bowl. Warm the milk and stir in the yeast, and leave until the yeast is frothing. Add to the dry ingredients with the warmed lard, cream and egg. Knead to a smooth dough. Cover and leave in a warm place for 45 minutes. Knead again and work in the currants. Shape into 18 small buns and place on a greased baking tray. Leave in a warm place for 10 minutes. Meanwhile preheat oven to 400°F/200°C/Gas Mark 6. Bake for 25 minutes. Cool on a wire rack and sprinkle with sieved icing sugar.

West Country Splits

These buns are like a light sweet bread and are split and filled with jam and whipped cream. They are a speciality of Devon and Cornwall, possibly because there was always rich cream to spare and it could be used to transform an otherwise plain bun.

12 oz (350 g) bread flour
Pinch of salt
1½ oz (40 g) sugar
1½ oz (40 g) butter
½ oz (15 g) fresh yeast *or* ¼ oz (7 g) dried yeast
½ pt (300 ml) water
4 oz (100 g) strawberry *or* raspberry jam
½ pt (300 ml) double cream
Icing sugar for sprinkling

Grease a baking sheet. Sieve the flour and salt into a warm bowl and stir in the sugar. Rub in the butter. Heat the water and cream the yeast with a little of it, then add the remaining water and leave until the yeast is frothing. Mix into the flour to form a firm dough. Cover and leave in a warm place for 45 minutes. Knead well and shape into eighteen buns. Put on the baking sheet and leave in a warm place for 10 minutes. Meanwhile, preheat the oven to 450°F/230°C/Gas Mark 8. Bake for 15 minutes. Cool on a wire rack. Split the buns diagonally almost to the base. Spread the opening generously with jam and fill with whipped cream. Dust with sieved icing sugar.

Hot Cross Buns

In medieval times all bread was marked with a cross to ward off evil spirits. This practice was condemned by the Puritans as being 'popish' and only the buns eaten hot on Good Friday retained the mark as a sign of the Crucifixion. Saffron or Revel Buns (pp. 38) were thought to be the originals of today's Hot Cross Buns, but today's bun omits the saffron and is not quite so rich. The cross may be cut with a knife or marked with marzipan or pastry, but many professional bakers use a thin wafer cross. These buns were traditionally eaten hot early in the morning, and in many areas they were distributed by charities to needy families. Sometimes a bun was saved for good luck and it was said that a Hot Cross Bun would just get very hard, but would never go mouldy. In country districts some families had collections of buns dating back over many years.

Batter
4 oz (100 g) bread flour
¼ pt (150 ml) milk
¼ pt (150 ml) water
1 oz (25 g) fresh yeast *or* ½ oz (15 g) dried yeast

Dough
12 oz (350 g) bread flour
1 tsp salt
½ tsp ground mixed spice
½ tsp ground cinnamon
½ tsp ground nutmeg
2 oz (50 g) sugar
2 oz (50 g) butter
1 egg
4 oz (100 g) currants
2 oz (50 g) chopped mixed candied peel

Glaze
2 tbsp milk
2 tbsp water
1¼ oz (40 g) sugar

Put the flour for the batter into a warm bowl. Heat the milk and water and mix with the yeast, and leave until the yeast is frothing. Mix into the flour and leave until the mixture is light and bubbling. To make the dough, sieve together the flour, salt and spices and stir in the sugar. Melt the butter, cool and add to the batter with the beaten egg. Work into the dry ingredients with the currants and peel. Work into a soft dough. Cover and leave in a warm place for 1 hour. Divide the dough into twelve pieces and shape into buns. Arrange on a greased baking sheet, cover and leave in a warm place for 30 minutes. Cut across with a sharp knife to form a cross, or top with a thin cross of marzipan or shortcrust pastry (2 oz (50 g) will be enough). Meanwhile preheat oven to 425°F/220°C/Gas Mark 7. Bake for 20 minutes. To make the glaze, boil the milk, water and sugar together until the sugar has dissolved. Remove buns from oven and brush over at once with the glaze. Cool on a wire rack.

Teacakes

This flat, saucer-sized bun is delicious freshly baked, but is much appreciated split, toasted and heavily buttered. The teacake used to be the focal point of tea on British Rail trains, but has sadly been replaced by a small, inferior and poorly fruited bun.

Dough
8 oz (225 g) bread flour
½ oz (15 g) butter
1 oz (25 g) sugar
1½ oz (40 g) mixed dried fruit
¼ pt (150 ml) milk
½ oz (15 g) fresh yeast *or* ¼ oz (7 g) dried yeast
1 egg

Glaze
1 tsp sugar
2 tbsp milk

Sieve the flour into a warm bowl and rub in the butter. Stir in the sugar and dried fruit. Warm the milk and mix with the yeast. When the yeast is frothing, pour into the dry ingredients. Add the egg and mix to a soft dough. Cover with a cloth and leave in a warm place for 45 minutes. Knead well until smooth and divide into 3 pieces. Shape into flat round cakes and put on a greased baking sheet. Cover and leave in a warm place for 10 minutes. Preheat oven to 450°F/230°C/Gas Mark 8. Bake for 12 minutes. Meanwhile, stir the sugar into the milk until dissolved. When the hot cakes come from the oven, brush over with this glaze.

Caraway Seed Bread

2 lb (900 g) bread flour
1½ tsp salt
3 tsp caraway seeds
1 tsp light soft brown sugar
2 oz (50 g) lard
1 pt (600 ml) water
1 oz (25 g) fresh yeast *or* ½ oz (15 g) dried yeast

Grease a baking sheet. Sieve the flour and salt into a warm bowl. Stir in the caraway seeds and sugar and rub in the lard. Heat the water and mix a little with the yeast then add the remaining water and leave until the dough is frothing. Work into the dry ingredients to form a soft dough. Cover and leave in a warm place for 1 hour. Knead well and form into two round loaves. Put on to the baking sheet and leave in a warm place for 45 minutes. Meanwhile preheat the oven to 400°F/200°C/Gas Mark 6. Bake for 40 minutes. Cool on a wire rack. Serve sliced and buttered.

Caraway Buns

These buns are shaped like flat teacakes and will keep moist for a week. They are good toasted, or may be quickly rebaked after dipping into warm milk. Caraway has a particularly good flavour when eaten hot.

½ pt (300 ml) milk
3 oz (75 g) golden syrup
1 oz (25 g) fresh yeast *or* ½ oz (15 g) dried yeast
1 lb (450 g) wholemeal bread flour
8 oz (225 g) white bread flour
1 tsp salt
½ oz (15 g) caraway seeds
1 oz (25 g) butter

Grease four 7 in. (17.5 cm) sponge sandwich tins. Warm the milk and stir in the golden syrup and then the yeast. Leave until the yeast is frothing. Sieve the flours and salt into a warm bowl. Mix in the yeast liquid and knead well. Add the caraway seeds and knead again. Cover and leave in a warm place for 1 hour. Knead well and divide between the sponge tins. Cover and leave in a warm place for 45 minutes. Preheat oven to 450°F/230°C/Gas Mark 8. Bake for 15 minutes. Melt the butter and brush the tops of the buns. Return to the oven for 15 minutes. Serve hot, split and buttered.

Sally Lunn

The name of this sweet plain loaf is said to derive from the Bath pastrycook who first made it in the late eighteenth century and whose house still stands in Lilliput Alley. Another version of the story is that the name derives from the cry 'Soleil Lune' (sun-and-moon) because the loaf was rounded and golden on top but pale underneath.

12 oz (350 g) bread flour
½ tsp salt
¼ pt (150 ml) milk
½ oz (15 g) fresh yeast *or* ¼ oz (7 g) dried yeast
1½ oz (40 g) sugar
2 oz (50 g) butter
1 egg
Grated rind of 1 lemon
Beaten egg

Grease two 6 in. (15 cm) round cake tins or straight-sided soufflé dishes. Sieve the flour and salt into a warm bowl. Warm the milk and mix with the yeast and leave until the yeast is frothing. Stir into the dry ingredients with the sugar. Melt the butter, cool slightly and add to the mixture with the egg and lemon rind. Mix well to a soft dough. Cover and leave in a warm place for 45 minutes. Knead again and divide into two pieces. Fit into the prepared tins, cover and leave in a warm place for 30 minutes.

Meanwhile, preheat oven to 450°F/230°C/Gas Mark 8. Brush with beaten egg. Bake for 30 minutes. Turn out and cool for 10 minutes. Split the loaves across into four layers and spread thickly with butter. Put together the layers and cut into wedges. Cover with a damp cloth and leave in the cooling oven until the butter has melted. Serve at once.

Selkirk Bannock

The name 'bannock' is said to derive from the Latin 'panicum' or bread, and this cake-bread looks like a large flat loaf. It was originally baked on a griddle and was usually a form of oatcake, but special forms were prepared for celebrations, such as the Bride's Bannock, or the curious Beltane Bannock made for the first day of summer on 1 May. This bannock was topped by nine square knobs, each dedicated to a supposed preserver of flocks and herds. Each person had to turn his face to the fire, break off a knob and fling it over his shoulder as an offering to the gods to save the animals, or to beg mercy from predators such as foxes or crows who might harm them. This is thought to be a relic of a similar pagan custom in Ancient Greece. The rich Selkirk Bannock was first prepared in the middle of the nineteenth century by Robert Douglas at Selkirk Market.

1 lb (450 g) sultanas
1 lb (450 g) bread flour
1 tsp salt
3 oz (75 g) butter
3 oz (75 g) sugar
½ pt (300 ml) milk
1 oz (25 g) fresh yeast *or* ½ oz (15 g) dried yeast
Beaten egg

Put the sultanas into a bowl and just cover with boiling water. Leave to stand for 30 minutes, drain well and dry carefully with kitchen paper. Grease two baking sheets. Sieve the flour and salt into a warm bowl, and rub in the butter. Stir in the sugar. Warm the milk and mix a little with the yeast, then add the remaining milk until the yeast is frothing. Add to the dried ingredients and mix thoroughly to a soft dough. Cover and leave in a warm place for 30 minutes. Knead in the sultanas carefully as they will be very soft. Cover and leave in a warm place for 15 minutes. Divide the dough into three pieces and shape into three balls. Place on baking sheet, cover and leave in a warm place for 45 minutes. Flatten the balls with the hand and brush lightly with beaten egg. Cover and leave to rise for 45 minutes. Meanwhile, preheat oven to 425°F/220°C/Gas Mark 7. Bake for 25 minutes. Cool on a wire rack.

Saffron Cake

It is said that saffron was introduced to Cornwall by Phoenician traders who exchanged it with other spices for tin. Certainly the golden stamens have coloured buns and cakes for centuries in the West Country, although the great centre for growing English saffron was in north-west Essex. The town of Chipping Walden became Saffron Walden, and the purple crocus remains part of the town's crest. Although the saffron cake does not seem to be sold in that area, I have heard rumours of oval-shaped saffron buns like Hot Cross Buns still being made in Saffron Walden and Thaxted, but have never tracked them down. Saffron Buns were often known as Sunday Buns in the West Country because they were made for special occasions. Saffron bread or cake is traditionally made for Easter and is thought to be the pre-Reformation Lenten bread to which sugar, rosewater and currants were later added, but it became a treat to be eaten on any festive occasion. It is meant to be sliced and eaten with butter, or, better still, clotted cream. The stamens of the saffron crocus (*crocus sativus*) cost about £500 for 2 lb (1 kg), which represents 500,000 flowers, so it is an expensive spice, and not widely used in this country today, but may be bought from good grocers or spice shops. To obtain the best flavour, the stamens or 'strands' should be left in water overnight. To speed up the process, they may be steeped in hot water or milk for 30 minutes, and the strained coloured liquid is then used.

½ pt (300 ml) milk
½ tsp saffron strands
½ oz (15 g) fresh yeast *or* ¼ oz (7 g) dried yeast
3 oz (75 g) caster sugar
1 lb (450 g) bread flour
6 oz (150 g) butter
6 oz (150 g) currants
2 oz (50 g) chopped mixed candied peel

Grease an 8 in. (20 cm) round cake tin. Boil the milk and put in the saffron. Leave to stand for 30 minutes. Strain, reheat the milk and mix with the yeast. Leave until the yeast is frothing. Stir the sugar and flour together and rub in the butter until the mixture is like fine crumbs. Add the yeast liquid and work to a soft dough. Stir in the currants and peel, cover and leave to stand for 1 hour. Preheat oven to 350°F/180°C/Gas Mark 4. Knead the dough and shape to fit the prepared tin. Bake for 1 hour. Leave to cool in tin. Serve fresh with butter or cream.

Pembroke Harvest Cakes

Not so long ago the harvest was a long and dusty business. Teams of men, women and horses cut the corn while children helped with 'stooking' or standing the sheaves in a kind of pyramid. When the sheaves had dried, they had to be loaded on carts and taken to the threshing floor where the grain was beaten from the chaff. The harvest went on from July to September, and children had a long holiday from school because they were an important part of the farm labour force. Since the daylight hours were precious meals were taken to the fields by the workers, or brought out later by their womenfolk, and the meals rejoiced in many different names such as 'baggins', 'snaps', 'elevenses' and 'fourses'. The meal might be some kind of stew kept warm in a covered basket, a pie or pastry, or sandwiches, washed down with long draughts of cold tea. Snacks were often some kind of simple bun or cake, of which this is a Welsh example. The final harvest feast was the Horkey given by the farmer for his men when the last sheaves were carried home and everyone had time to drink and celebrate. Today's religious Harvest Festival is, however, a Victorian invention of a Cornish clergyman.

1½ lb (675 g) bread flour
Pinch of salt
1 oz (25 g) fresh yeast *or* ½ oz (7 g) dried yeast
¾ pt (450 ml) milk
3 oz (75 g) light soft brown sugar
4 oz (100 g) beef dripping
6 oz (150 g) seedless raisins or sultanas

Sieve the flour and salt into a warm bowl. Mix the yeast with a little warm milk and add to the remaining lukewarm milk. When the yeast is frothing, mix with the flour and stir in the sugar. Beat well and add melted dripping. When thoroughly blended, stir in the dried fruit. Knead lightly, cover with a cloth and leave in a warm place for 45 minutes. Dust a board with flour and sugar and knead the mixture until smooth. Divide into 4 pieces and shape into flat cakes. Put on to two greased baking sheets, cover and leave to stand for 15 minutes. Preheat oven to 425°F/220°C/Gas Mark 7. Cut each circle into four wedges with a sharp knife, and separate slightly. Bake for 10 minutes. Reduce heat to 350°F/180°C/Gas Mark 4 and continue baking for 25 minutes.

Yule Bread

Before cake became popular when ovens were widely introduced at the end of the eighteenth century, a fruited bread was traditional as the bread could be baked by the village baker. This fruit loaf still remains popular in the North Country and in Wales where customs have lingered. The bread was made at least two weeks before Christmas, and was often 'fed' with ale about a week after baking to improve its texture and flavour.

Batter
5 tbsp milk
1 egg
1 oz (25 g) sugar
½ oz (15 g) fresh yeast *or* ¼ oz (7 g) dried yeast
2 oz (50 g) bread flour

Dough
4 oz (100 g) lard
4 oz (100 g) dark soft brown sugar
1 tbsp black treacle
1 egg
8 oz (225 g) bread flour
2 tsp baking powder
1 tsp salt
1 tsp ground nutmeg
2 tsp ground mixed spice
8 oz (225 g) currants
4 oz (100 g) sultanas
1 oz (25 g) chopped mixed candied peel

Grease and base-line a 2 lb (900 g) loaf tin. Prepare the batter by heating the milk and mixing with the egg, sugar, yeast and flour. Cover and leave to stand in a warm place for 30 minutes. Prepare the dough by creaming the lard and sugar and working in the treacle and egg. Sieve the flour with the baking powder, salt and spices, and work into the creamed mixture. Add the batter. Mix very thoroughly and add the dried fruit and peel. Work to a soft smooth dough. Place in the prepared tin, cover and leave in a warm place for 45 minutes. Meanwhile, preheat oven to 400°F/200°C/Gas Mark 6. Bake for 1 hour. Cool on a wire rack, wrap and store in a tin. If liked, prick the base with a skewer after a week's storage and spoon over a little Guinness or strong ale.

Victorian Dough Cake

Liquid ale yeast or 'barm' was used for cakes until well into the eighteenth century before cooks discovered the way in which eggs could be used as a raising agent. Later ammonia was used, but baking powder and self-raising flour were Victorian inventions. A yeast-raised cake often appeared in nineteenth-century recipe books however, but by then the yeast was a more easily handled compressed cake. This cake is a good example of the sort of thing which was prepared. It is rather more solid than today's fruit cakes.

10 oz (300 g) bread flour
2 oz (50 g) fine semolina *or* ground rice
8 oz (225 g) mixed dried fruit
3 oz (75 g) sugar
3 oz (75 g) butter or lard
1 oz (25 g) fresh yeast *or* ½ oz (15 g) dried yeast
¼ pt (150 ml) milk
2 eggs

Grease and line a 7 in. (17.5 cm) round cake tin. Stir together the flour, semolina or rice, dried fruit and sugar. Rub in the fat and the yeast. Warm the milk slightly and add to the dry ingredients with the eggs and knead well together. Cover and leave in a warm place for 45 minutes. Meanwhile preheat oven to 400°F/200°C/Gas Mark 6. Bake for 1 hour. Cool in tin for 5 minutes, then turn out and cool on a wire rack. Eat freshly baked.

Lardy Cake

This countrywide favourite was derived from bread dough wrapped in layers around lard, sugar and dried fruit, since most people made bread and kept a pig. It is particularly associated with Wiltshire and Gloucestershire, traditionally associated with the pig industry. There is a Suffolk version which omits the fruit and is called Brotherly Love, and there is also an old Wiltshire version with caraway seeds, but most people now think of Lardy Cake as being well stuffed with plenty of dried fruit. If bread dough is available, this may be used, but many people are happy to make a special dough for the cake.

8 oz (225 g) bread flour
¼ tsp salt
¼ tsp ground mixed spice
¼ pt (150 ml) milk
¼ oz (25 g) fresh yeast *or* 1 tsp dried yeast
2 oz (50 g) lard
2 oz (50 g) sugar
3 oz (75 g) mixed dried fruit

Grease a 7 in. (17.5 cm) square cake tin. Sieve the flour, salt and spice into a bowl. Warm the milk and mix with the yeast and leave until the yeast is frothing. Add to the dry ingredients and mix to a soft dough. Cover and leave in a warm place for 45 minutes. Roll out ¼ in. (65 mm) thick and spread on half the lard, sugar and fruit. Fold in three, turn to left and roll out again. Repeat with remaining lard, sugar and fruit, fold and shape into the cake tin. Cover and leave in a warm place for 1 hour. Meanwhile preheat oven to 450°F/230°C/Gas Mark 8. Score the top of the cake with a knife to make diamonds and brush with a little sugar dissolved in water. Bake for 30 minutes. Leave in tin for 10 minutes, then put on to a wire rack to cool. Spoon any syrup from the base of the tin over the cake. Serve freshly baked, or sliced, toasted and buttered.

Lincolnshire Whitsun Cake

This is an interesting and very rich version of the Lardy Cake made from bread dough layered with sugar, fat and dried fruit. Since a lot of butter and sugar is used, the effect is more like a very rich Danish Pastry. Originally, the cake was baked like a loaf without a tin, but as it can be a little messy it is easier to put it into a round cake tin.

7 oz (200 g) butter
12 oz (350 g) bread flour
Pinch of salt
½ oz (15 g) fresh yeast *or* ¼ oz (7 g) dried yeast
¼ pt (150 ml) milk
8 oz (225 g) currants
8 oz (225 g) light soft brown sugar
Pinch of ground nutmeg
Pinch of ground allspice
1 egg

Grease an 8 in. (20 cm) round cake tin. Preheat oven to 400°F/200°C/Gas Mark 6. Rub 3 oz (75 g) butter into the flour and salt. Sprinkle the yeast on to warm milk and leave until frothy. Add to the flour with 3 oz (75 g) melted butter. Knead to a soft dough, cover and leave to prove for 45 minutes. Meanwhile, mix the currants, sugar, spices and remaining butter in a saucepan and simmer for 10 minutes. Leave until cool and beat in the egg yolk. Divide the dough into 4 pieces and roll out to fit the cake tin. Place one piece in the tin and top with one third currant mixture. Add another piece of dough, one-third currant mixture, more dough and the remaining currant mixture. Top with the remaining dough, and seal the edges firmly with a little of the egg white. Bake for 45 minutes. Brush over with remaining egg white and continue baking for 10 minutes. Turn on to a wire rack to cool. The cake is best if kept in a tin for 2–3 days before eating so that the flavour of the filling goes through the dough layers.

Yeast Wigs

Wigs were ceremonial cakes served with mulled ale or elderberry wine on special occasions (p. 145). This is probably the original way of making them with yeast, although later versions were raised by other agents.

1 lb bread flour
1 tsp ground mixed spice
Pinch of salt
¼ oz (7 g) caraway seeds
2 oz (50 g) sugar
½ pt (300 ml) milk
½ oz (15 g) fresh yeast *or* ¼ oz (7 g) dried yeast
2 oz (50 g) butter

Grease a baking sheet. Sieve the flour, spice and salt into a warm bowl.

Stir in the caraway seeds and sugar. Warm the milk and use a little to cream the yeast, then add the remaining milk and leave until the yeast is frothing. Add to the flour and mix well. Melt the butter and work into the mixture to make a soft smooth dough. Cover and leave in a warm place for 45 minutes. Knead well and roll out on a floured board into two 7 in. (17.5 cm) rounds. Cut each into 4 or 8 wedges. Place on the baking sheet and leave in a warm place for 20 minutes. Meanwhile, preheat oven to 450°F/230°C/Gas Mark 8. Bake for 20 minutes. Serve freshly baked, and eat after dipping into the hot ale or wine.

Lancashire Cakes

These cakes may be the original version of the Eccles Cakes which enclose dried fruit in a pastry case, which is here substituted by a yeast dough. They are a delicious form of bun and are best eaten when freshly baked.

1 lb (450 g) bread flour
1 tsp salt
½ oz (15 g) lard
½ pt (300 ml) water
½ oz (15 g) fresh yeast *or* ¼ oz (7 g) dried yeast
6 oz (150 g) currants
2 oz (50 g) chopped mixed candied peel
1 oz (25 g) light soft brown sugar
Pinch of ground nutmeg

Grease two baking sheets. Sieve the flour and salt into a warm bowl and rub in the lard. Warm the water and mix a little with the yeast then add the remaining water and leave until the yeast is frothing. Add to the dry ingredients and mix to a smooth dough. Cover and leave in a warm place for 45 minutes. Knead again, and roll out the dough and cut into circles round the edge of a tea plate. Sprinkle the centre of each circle with currants, peel, sugar and nutmeg. Join the edges of the pastry and pinch them together. Turn over each cake and roll lightly into circles. Put on to the baking sheets and prick well with a fork. Leave in a warm place for 15 minutes. Meanwhile preheat oven to 425°F/220°C/Gas Mark 7. Bake for 20 minutes. Cool on a wire rack.

Shropshire Soul Cakes

These cakes were distributed on All Souls' Day 2 November until about 1850, when children used to sing at people's doors and ask for a gift of money, buns or something to drink. They sang:

> Soul, soul, for a soul-cake,
> Pray good missus – a soul-cake,
> One for Peter, two for Paul.

As the soul-cake was eaten, it was important to say 'A soul-cake, a soul-cake, have mercy on all Christian souls.' In parts of Shropshire and Cheshire children still go 'souling' at the end of October, singing from house to house and collecting money, but in other areas the custom has merged with the pagan 'trick' or 'treat' of Hallowe'en (the eve of All Saints' Day which occurs in the Church calendar on the day before All Souls'). The earliest version of the cake, given here, uses yeast and is without fruit. Another type of Soul Cake is coloured and flavoured with saffron, has no raising agent, but contains currants.

1½ lb (675 g) white bread flour
4 oz (100 g) butter
½ oz (15 g) fresh yeast *or* ¼ oz (7 g) dried yeast
½ pt (300 ml) milk
1 egg
4 oz (100 g) sugar
½ tsp ground allspice

Sieve the flour and rub in the butter until the mixture is like fine breadcrumbs. Mix the fresh yeast with a teaspoon of sugar and add to warm milk (or sprinkle dried yeast on the milk). When the yeast is foaming, add to the flour with the egg and mix well to form a light dough, adding a little extra milk if necessary. Put into an oiled bowl, cover and leave in a warm place for 45 minutes until light and puffy. Work in the sugar and spice and form into round buns. Place on a greased baking sheet, cover and leave to rise in a warm place for 15 minutes. Mark across the tops with a cross. Bake at 425°F/220°C/Gas Mark 7 for 15 minutes. Cool on a wire rack.

Doughnuts

Fried cakes were some of the earliest treats which could easily be prepared before ovens came into common use, and they occur all over the world. A plain bread dough was nearly always being prepared in the kitchen, and it was an easy matter to pinch off small pieces and to fry them in hot fat to make a quick cake. The traditional version is always filled with red jam and tossed in caster sugar.

8 oz (225 g) bread flour
Pinch of salt
1 oz (25 g) butter
1 oz (25 g) sugar
¼ pt (150 ml) milk
1 egg
½ oz (15 g) fresh yeast *or* ¼ oz (7 g) dried yeast
Jam
Oil for frying
Caster sugar for sprinkling

Sieve the flour and salt into a warm basin and rub in the butter. Stir in the sugar. Warm the milk and dissolve the yeast in it, leaving until the yeast is frothing. Add to the flour with the egg, and mix well, kneading thoroughly to a smooth dough. Cover and leave in a warm place for 45 minutes. Knead again and form into 12 balls. Poke a hole in each ball with a finger and put in a little jam. Reform the balls. Leave in a warm place for 10 minutes. Fry in hot oil until golden, drain and toss in caster sugar.

Isle of Wight Doughnuts

2 lb (900 g) bread flour
2 oz (50 g) lard
4 oz (100 g) caster sugar
1 tsp ground allspice
Pinch of ground cinnamon
Pinch of ground cloves
Pinch of ground nutmeg
½ pt (300 ml) milk
1 oz (25 g) fresh yeast *or* ½ oz (15 g) dried yeast
1 oz (25 g) currants
Oil for frying
Caster sugar for sprinkling

Sieve the flour into a warm bowl and rub in the lard until the mixture is like fine breadcrumbs. Stir in the sugar and spices. Warm the milk and add the yeast and leave until frothy. Add to the flour and knead to a firm dough. Cover and leave in a warm place for 1½ hours. Knead again and form into balls about the size of a small apple. Poke a hole in each ball with a finger and put in a few currants and then reform the balls. Leave in a warm place for 10 minutes. Fry in hot oil until golden, drain and toss in caster sugar.

Oast Cakes

Kent is a county famous for its fruit and hops and the countryside is dotted with low round towers which have conical roofs. These hop kilns or oast houses were designed for drying hops, although many of them have now been converted into houses. The following recipe is for an unusual little fried cake which is another example of the quickly prepared treats once made for agricultural workers, in this case hop pickers and processors.

8 oz (225 g) plain flour
1 tsp baking powder
Pinch of salt
1 oz (25 g) sugar
2 oz (50 g) lard
3 oz (75 g) currants
Squeeze of lemon juice
Water
Oil for frying
Caster sugar for sprinkling

Sieve the flour, baking powder and salt into a bowl. Stir in the sugar and rub in the lard. Add the currants and a squeeze of lemon juice. Add just enough water to make a firm dough. Pinch off pieces of dough about the size of a large walnut. Form into a ball and then flatten slightly with a rolling pin. Fry the cakes in hot oil until golden on both sides. Drain well and sprinkle with caster sugar. Eat the cakes when freshly cooked.

Northumberland Twists

1 lb (450 g) bread flour
4 oz (100 g) caster sugar
4 oz (100 g) butter
¼ pt (150 ml) water
½ oz (15 g) fresh yeast *or* ¼ oz (7 g) dried yeast
3 tbsp medium sherry
Caster sugar for sprinkling

Grease two baking sheets. Stir the flour and sugar together in a warm bowl. Melt the butter, cool slightly and work into the dough. Warm the water and mix 2–3 tablespoons with the yeast. Add to the flour mixture with enough warm water to make a firm dough. Knead until smooth, cover and leave in a warm place for two hours. Preheat oven to 375°F/190°C/Gas Mark 5. Knead the dough well again and then roll out on a floured board. Cut out strips about 4 in. (10 cm) long and 1½ in. (3.75 cm) wide. Twist slightly and put on to baking sheets. Brush well with sherry and sprinkle with caster sugar. Bake for 20 minutes. Eat freshly baked.

5 Gingerbreads, Honey Cakes and Spice Cakes

> On her way home, she usually bought a slice of honey-cake at the baker's. It was her Sunday treat. Sometimes there was an almond in her slice, sometimes not. It made a great difference. If there was an almond it was like carrying home a tiny present – a surprise – something that might very well not have been there.
>
> (Katherine Mansfield, *Short Stories*)

It is said that gingerbread is the oldest form of cake in the world, originally prepared by a Greek baker in Rhodes, but certainly spice breads have been popular for thousands of years. Honey and spices were introduced to Britain by the Romans, but were not used in bread but as a softener and sweetener, rather as liquid honey is still poured over cakes and pastries from the Middle East. The first spice cakes seem to have been medieval mixtures deriving from sloppy potages and consisting of breadcrumbs mixed with honey, pepper, saffron and cinnamon. This mixture was made into a stiff paste which could be shaped into a block, then sliced and coloured red with sandalwood, or decorated with box leaves impaled by the nails of cloves. This method was still given by Sir Hugh Plat in 1609 in *Delights for Ladies* when fine white bread or 'manchet' was used. The bread was grated, then dried and the crumbs sieved. A flavouring of ginger, cinnamon, liquorice and aniseed was added, and the whole sweetened with sugar and mixed with claret. This gingerbread was then rolled thinly and pressed into moulds dusted with cinnamon, ginger and liquorice.

The range of spices included in gingerbread was very varied and some old recipes even omit the ginger. Pepper is sometimes recorded and the cake is often known as peppercake, but it is possible that allspice was intended, since it was also known as Jamaica pepper. The early Spanish explorers mistook the tiny round berries for pepper and called it pimenta after *pimentia*, the Spanish word for pepper. Since allspice combines the flavour of nutmeg, cinnamon and cloves, it would have been a natural choice for spice cakes. Certainly the modern cook will find that a mixture of spices gives a much better flavour to gingerbread than just ginger alone.

Treacle was introduced into England in the seventeenth century and became a cheap and popular substitute for honey, making the gingerbread into a lighter cake, although the moulded variety remained popular as a fairing (Chapter Twelve) and became a kind of ginger biscuit. Countess Fitzwilliam in her eighteenth-century stillroom book recorded the new type of gingerbread:

> Take a pound and a half of fine flour and set it before ye fire to Dry then set to it a Qr. of an ounce of Cloves & nutmegs together and what

Corriander and Carroway Seeds you please Half an Ounce of Ginger finely beaten and sifted. Then take 4 egg and leave out 2 of ye whites. Beat ym and put ym into flower put into it one pound of sugar take 1 pound of butter 2 of Treacle and a quarter of a pint of Brandy. Sett all these on ye fire Untill ye Butter is melted then Mix all those together a moderate stiffness and when they are ready to fill your tins put into it a Quarter of a pound of Dry'd sweet meats Cut Small you must Butter ye sides of your pan.

The method of heating the treacle is not so different from today's preparation of gingerbread, but this is for a fine cake for the grand household at Wentworth Woodhouse in Yorkshire. Poorer cooks in the north were able to obtain treacle easily from the ports on the Lancashire and Cumberland coasts where it arrived from the West Indies, but they prepared a coarser mixture with oatmeal, since oats were the most easily grown cereal in a northern climate. This produced the solid parkin, so popular in Yorkshire and Lancashire, and considered to be a celebration cake at winter festivals.

Sticky Gingerbread

8 oz (225 g) margarine
8 oz (225 g) dark soft brown sugar
8 oz (225 g) black treacle
12 oz (350 g) plain flour
4 tsp ground ginger
3 tsp ground cinnamon
2 eggs
½ pt (300 ml) milk
2 tsp bicarbonate of soda

Grease and line a 12 × 8 in. (30 × 20 cm) cake tin. Preheat oven to 325°F/160°C/Gas mark 3. Put the margarine, sugar and treacle into a pan and heat gently until melted. Sieve the flour, ginger and cinnamon together and stir in the melted mixture. Beat the eggs and stir into the mixture. Warm the milk just to blood heat and add the soda. Pour into the cake mixture, beat well and pour into the tin. Bake for 1½ hours. Cool in the tin for 10 minutes, then turn on to a wire rack to cool.

Honey Cake

Honey has been a favourite food since prehistoric times when honey-gatherers had to tackle the nests of wild bees. By the late Bronze Age these collectors cut away a section of hollow tree where bees had swarmed and took it back to a bee garden near their dwelling. Later hives were constructed from bark or wickerwork and smeared with honey and herbs to encourage bees to occupy them. Sugar was cultivated in India from the seventh century but was really only introduced to Europe in the twelfth century by returning Crusaders. It remained a luxury until the early eighteenth century when imports rose and even the poorest people could afford to use a little. Beekeeping remained a favourite country pastime, and when anyone died in a beekeeping family it was the custom for the nearest relative to 'whisper to the bees' and tell them of the death. If this custom should be neglected, the precious bees would desert the hives.

2 oz (50 g) butter
5 oz (125 g) clear honey
5 oz (125 g) demerara sugar
10 oz (300 g) plain flour
Pinch of salt
1 tsp bicarbonate of soda
1 tsp ground mixed spice
1 tsp ground ginger
1 tsp ground cinnamon
4 oz (100 g) chopped mixed candied peel
1 egg
¼ pt (150 ml) milk
1 oz (25 g) flaked almonds

Grease a 1 lb (450 g) loaf tin. Preheat oven to 350°F/180°C/Gas Mark 4. Put the butter into a saucepan and heat gently until just melted. Remove from the heat and stir in the honey and sugar. Mix well and leave until lukewarm. Sift the flour, salt, soda, spice, ginger and cinnamon, and stir in the peel. Beat the egg and milk together and add to the honey. Pour this liquid into the flour and beat until smooth. Pour the cake mixture into the tin and scatter on the almonds very lightly. Bake for 1¼ hours. Cool in the tin for 5 minutes, then turn out on to a wire rack to cool. Serve sliced and buttered.

Yorkshire Parkin

This dark solid gingerbread keeps very well and this has led to the Yorkshire saying to anyone who is ill 'don't worry, you'll soon be like a parkin'. The cake is traditionally eaten on Guy Fawkes night, 5 November, which is celebrated with great bonfires in the county where Guy Fawkes was born. This has always been a popular festival as it was so close in time to the more ancient fire festival of Hallowe'en and was one of the few which the Puritans allowed to continue in the seventeenth century. A similar cake is eaten in Lancashire at Hallowe'en under the name of Harcake or Soul Mass Cake. A parkin needs to be made in advance as it should be kept in a tin for at least a week before eating. Yorkshiremen like to eat this cake with a piece of Wensleydale cheese.

6 oz (150 g) plain flour
1 tsp salt
2 tsp ground ginger
1 tsp ground cinnamon
1 tsp ground nutmeg
1 tsp bicarbonate of soda
10 oz (350 g) medium oatmeal
6 oz (150 g) black treacle
5 oz (125 g) butter
4 oz (100 g) dark soft brown sugar
¼ pt (150 ml) milk
1 egg

Grease and line a 7 in. (17.5 cm) square cake tin. Preheat oven to 350°F/180°C/Gas Mark 4. Sift together the flour, salt, spices and soda. Stir in the oatmeal and toss lightly to mix. Put the treacle, butter, sugar and milk into a saucepan and heat gently until the butter has melted. Cool to lukewarm. Beat in the egg. Pour the liquid mixture into the dry ingredients and beat well until smooth. Pour into the cake tin. Bake for 1 hour. Cool in the tin for 5 minutes, then turn out on a wire rack to finish cooling. Store in a tin for a week before cutting.

Colchester Gingerbread

At Colchester (Essex) a feast of gin and gingerbread has traditionally celebrated the opening of the oyster season each year.

8 oz (225 g) butter or margarine
8 oz (225 g) dark soft brown sugar
8 oz (225 g) black treacle
12 oz (350 g) plain flour
4 tsp ground ginger
3 tsp ground cinnamon
2 eggs
½ pt (300 ml) milk
2 tsp bicarbonate of soda.

Grease and line a 12 × 8 in. (30 × 20 cm) tin. Preheat oven to 300°F/150°C/Gas Mark 2. Put the butter or margarine, sugar and treacle into a saucepan and heat gently until the fat has melted. Sift the flour, ginger and cinnamon together and pour in the treacle mixture. Add the beaten eggs and beat the mixture together until evenly coloured. Put the milk into a saucepan and heat to lukewarm. Stir in the soda and pour into the cake mixture. Beat well and pour in to the cake tin. Bake for 1 hour 45 minutes. Cool in the tin for 5 minutes and then turn out on a wire rack to cool.

Inverness Gingerbread

12 oz (350 g) plain flour
4 oz (100 g) fine oatmeal
8 oz (225 g) butter
12 oz (350 g) black treacle
1 oz (25 g) chopped stem ginger
4 oz (100 g) chopped mixed candied peel
7 tbsp milk
1 tsp bicarbonate of soda

Grease and line an 11 × 8 in. (30 × 20 cm) tin. Preheat oven to 350°F/180°C/Gas Mark 4. Stir the flour and oatmeal together. Cream the butter until light and fluffy and work in the flour mixture. Warm the treacle so that it runs easily, and work into the flour with the ginger and the peel. Heat the milk until just warm and stir in the soda. Add to the mixture and beat well. Spoon into the prepared tin. Bake for 1 hour. Leave in the tin for 15 minutes, then turn out on a wire rack to cool.

Duke of Windsor Gingerbread

This loaf contains many of the ingredients of early gingerbread and is reputed to have been a favourite cake of the Duke of Windsor when a child. It is very good sliced and spread with unsalted butter.

8 oz (225 g) plain flour
4 oz (100 g) butter
4 oz (100 g) dark soft brown sugar
½ oz (15 g) ground ginger
½ tsp ground allspice
½ tsp ground caraway
4 oz (100 g) blanched chopped almonds
1 oz (25 g) chopped mixed candied peel
8 oz (225 g) black treacle
¼ tsp bicarbonate of soda
1 egg
2 tbsp milk

Grease and lightly flour a 2 lb (900 g) loaf tin. Preheat oven to 350°F/180°C/Gas Mark 4. Sieve the flour into a bowl and rub in the butter until the mixture is like fine breadcrumbs. Stir in the sugar, spices, almonds and peel. Warm the treacle slightly until it is just thin and runny, but not hot. Stir in the soda and beat into the mixture. Beat the egg and milk lightly and stir into the mixture until well blended. Pour into the tin and bake for 40 minutes. Cool in the tin for 5 minutes, then turn on to a wire rack to cool.

Orange Gingerbread

This is a good recipe for those who enjoy ginger cakes, but do not like the strong flavour of black treacle.

12 oz (350 g) plain flour
½ tsp ground ginger
½ tsp ground cinnamon
½ tsp bicarbonate of soda
Pinch of salt
Pinch of cayenne pepper
4 oz (100 g) butter
4 oz (100 g) light soft brown sugar
4 oz (100 g) golden syrup
2 eggs
½ orange
3 oz (75 g) chopped candied orange peel

Grease and lightly flour a 7 in. (17.5 cm) round cake tin. Preheat oven to 325°F/160°C/Gas Mark 3. Sieve together the flour, spices, soda, salt and pepper. Rub in the butter until the mixture is like fine breadcrumbs. Stir in the sugar. Heat the syrup until it is just thin and runny and stir into the mixture. Whisk the eggs lightly and beat into the cake mixture. Grate the rind and squeeze the juice from the orange. Add to the mixture with the candied peel. Pour into the tin and bake for 1 hour. Leave in the tin for 5 minutes, then turn on to a wire rack to cool.

Old Welsh Gingerbread

The odd thing about this recipe is that it contains no ginger, but this was the traditional way to make 'gingerbread' for sale at Welsh fairs. It is a good rich cake anyway, but a heaped teaspoon of ground ginger may be added if liked.

12 oz (350 g) plain flour
½ tsp bicarbonate of soda
1 tsp cream of tartar
4 oz (100 g) butter
6 oz (150 g) demerara sugar
2 oz (50 g) chopped mixed candied peel
6 oz (150 g) black treacle
¼ pt (150 ml) milk

Grease a 7 × 11 in. (17.5 × 27.5 cm) rectangular tin and line the base with greaseproof paper. Preheat oven to 325°F/160°C/Gas Mark 3. Sift together the flour, soda and cream of tartar. Rub in the butter until the mixture is like fine breadcrumbs. Stir in the sugar and peel. Warm the treacle and milk together and pour into the dry ingredients. Beat well and pour into the prepared tin. Bake for 1½ hours. Cool in tin for 10 minutes, then turn on to a wire rack to cool.

North Country Overnight Spice Cake

In the days when an oven had to be carefully controlled and the heat gradually lowered from bread temperature to that suitable to biscuits and cakes, the baking day had to be carefully planned. Often mixtures were prepared the night before so that they were certain to be ready when the correct temperature was achieved, and the raising agent had had sufficient time to 'work' the dough.

1 lb (450 g) plain flour
6 oz (150 g) lard
2 oz (50 g) unsalted butter
8 oz (225 g) caster sugar
4 oz (110 g) ground almonds
2 tsp ground mixed spice
2½ tsp bicarbonate of soda
8 oz (225 g) currants
8 oz (225 g) raisins
½ pt (300 ml) sour milk

Grease and line a 9 in. (22.5 cm) round cake tin. Rub the fat into the flour until the mixture is like fine breadcrumbs. Stir in the sugar, almonds, spice, soda and dried fruit. Mix to a soft dough with the milk and place in the prepared tin. Leave overnight. Preheat oven to 325°F/160°C/Gas Mark 3. Bake for 1 hour. Reduce the heat to 300°F/150°C/Gas Mark 2 and continue baking for 1½ hours. Leave in the tin for 10 minutes, then turn on to a wire rack to cool.

Orkney Broonie

This is a solid and sustaining gingerbread and it is thought that it's name derives from a Norse word for a thick bannock. Plain white flour may be used, but the wholemeal flour gives a nuttier texture.

6 oz (150 g) wholemeal flour
6 oz (150 g) medium oatmeal
4 oz (100 g) dark soft brown sugar
1 tsp ground ginger
1 tsp bicarbonate of soda
Pinch of salt
2 oz (50 g) butter
2 tbsp black treacle
1 egg
½ pt (300 ml) buttermilk *or* sour milk

Grease and line a 2 lb (900 g) loaf tin. Preheat oven to 325°F/160°C/Gas Mark 3. Put the flour, oatmeal, sugar, ginger, soda and salt into a bowl and stir until evenly coloured. Rub in the butter. Mix the treacle, egg and milk together and beat into the mixture to give a dropping consistency. Put into the prepared tin. Bake for 1½ hours. Leave in tin for 10 minutes, then turn on to a wire rack to cool. Serve sliced and spread with butter.

Fishguard Gingerbread

This gingerbread from Pembrokeshire is very light because it includes sour milk, and is therefore more attractive to those who do not care for a heavy gingerbread.

12 oz (350 g) self-raising flour
1 tsp ground ginger
½ tsp salt
4 oz (100 g) butter
3 oz (75 g) light soft brown sugar
1 egg
5 oz (125 g) black treacle
¼ pt (150 ml) sour milk
½ tsp bicarbonate of soda
5 oz (125 g) stoned raisins

Grease and base-line a 7 × 11 in. (17.5 × 27.5 cm) rectangular tin. Preheat oven to 350°F/180°C/Gas Mark 4. Sieve the flour, ginger and salt into a bowl. Cream the butter and sugar until light and fluffy. Work in the egg and treacle. Gradually add the flour, mixing well. Dissolve the soda in the milk and beat into the mixture. Stir in the raisins. Put into the prepared tin. Bake for 40 minutes. Leave in the tin for 15 minutes, then turn on to a wire rack to cool.

Fochabers Gingerbread

This is a particularly rich gingerbread with plenty of dried fruit which is filling. It makes an excellent picnic cake.

8 oz (225 g) butter
4 oz (100 g) light soft brown sugar
8 oz (225 g) black treacle
2 eggs
1 lb (460 g) plain flour
1 oz (25 g) ground mixed spice
½ oz (15 g) ground ginger
Pinch of ground cloves
Pinch of ground cinnamon
4 oz (100 g) currants
4 oz (100 g) sultanas
3 oz (75 g) chopped mixed candied peel
3 oz (75 g) ground almonds
1 tsp bicarbonate of soda
½ pt (300 ml) beer

Grease and line a 9 in. (22.5 cm) round cake tin. Preheat oven to 325°F/160°C/Gas Mark 3. Cream the butter and sugar until light and fluffy. Warm the treacle until it is just runny. Beat into the fat mixture and then beat in the eggs. Sieve the flour with the spices. Stir into the mixture with the dried fruit and ground almonds. Dissolve the soda in the beer and beat into the cake mixture. Put into the prepared cake tin. Bake for 2 hours. Leave in the tin for 15 minutes, then turn on to a wire rack to cool.

Grantham White Gingerbread

4 oz (100 g) butter
4 oz (100 g) caster sugar
1 egg
8 oz (225 g) plain flour
1 tsp bicarbonate of soda
1 oz (25 g) ground ginger

Grease and base-line a 7 in. (17.5 cm) square cake tin. Preheat oven to 350°F/180°C/Gas Mark 4. Cream the butter and sugar until light and fluffy. Separate the egg and beat in the egg yolk. Sieve the flour with the soda and ginger, and work into the creamed mixture. Whip the egg white to stiff peaks and fold into the mixture. Put into the prepared tin. Bake for 35 minutes.

Carol Singing Pepper Cake

In Scandinavia, spice cakes and gingerbreads are known as 'pepperkaka', and presumably gave their name to this Yorkshire cake which was traditionally given to carol-singers at Christmas.

1½ lb (675 g) plain flour
8 oz (225 g) butter
8 oz (225 g) dark soft brown sugar
1 oz (25 g) ground cloves
1½ lb (675 g) black treacle
4 eggs
1 tsp bicarbonate of soda
4 tbsp milk

Grease and base-line a large roasting tin (about 10 × 14 in./25 × 35 cm). Preheat oven to 325°F/160°C/Gas Mark 3. Rub the butter into the flour until the mixture is like fine breadcrumbs. Stir in the sugar and cloves. Warm the treacle slightly until it runs freely. Mix into the dry ingredients with the beaten eggs. Dissolve the soda in about 4 tablespoons milk and add to the mixture, beating well. Put into prepared tin. Bake for 1¾ hours. Cool in tin for 15 minutes, then turn on to a wire rack to cool. Like most spice cakes, this one is better if stored in a tin for a few days before eating.

Ginger Cake

5 oz (125 g) plain flour
5 oz (125 g) porridge oats
½ tsp salt
4 tsp ground ginger
1 tsp ground cinnamon
2 tsp baking powder
6 oz (150 g) dark soft brown sugar
6 tbsp black treacle
4 oz (100 g) butter *or* margarine
1 egg
½ pt (300 ml) milk
4 oz (100 g) sultanas
2 oz (50 g) blanched almonds

Grease and line a 7 in. (17.5 cm) round cake tin. Preheat oven to 350°F/180°C/Gas Mark 4. Stir together the flour, oats, salt, spices, baking powder and sugar. Put the treacle and fat into a pan and heat gently together until the fat melts. Stir into the dry ingredients. Beat the egg and milk together and beat into the mixture. Stir in the sultanas and almonds. Spoon into the tin. Bake for 1¼ hours. Leave in the tin for 15 minutes, then turn out on a wire rack to cool. Like all gingerbreads this cake matures with keeping, and may be placed in a storage tin two weeks before it is to be eaten.

Gingerbread Men

These are a traditional treat for children and they can enjoy making them with a little supervision. The shape may be cut around a cardboard pattern, but there are many cutters available now, including those for kings and queens. The old-fashioned gingerbread man had two currant eyes and three currant buttons, but at Christmas time it is fun to decorate them with icing features and clothes and to hang them on the tree.

5 oz (125 g) dark soft brown sugar
5 oz (125 g) black treacle
3½ oz (90 g) butter
1 egg
1¼ lb (550 g) plain flour
1 tsp ground ginger
1 tsp ground cinnamon
¼ tsp ground cloves
½ oz (15 g) bicarbonate of soda
Currants

Grease two baking sheets. Preheat oven to 325°F/160°C/Gas Mark 3. Heat the sugar and treacle together until hot and pour on to the butter. Beat well until the fat has melted. Cool slightly and beat in the egg. Sieve together the flour, spices and soda. Pour in the treacle mixture and work together to make a smooth dough. Roll out and cut into shapes. Place on baking sheets and decorate with currants. Bake for 20 minutes. Lift carefully on to a wire rack to cool.

Norfolk Ginger Cake

A simple ginger cake which is not too strongly flavoured for those who do not like the heavy richness of traditional ginger cakes.

6 oz (150 g) self-raising flour
2 tsp ground ginger
3 oz (75 g) butter
2½ oz (65 g) granulated sugar
2 tbsp golden syrup
1 egg
2 tbsp milk
½ tsp bicarbonate of soda

Grease and line a 6 in. (15 cm) round cake tin. Preheat oven to 350°F/180°C/Gas Mark 4. Sieve the flour and ginger together and rub in the butter until the mixture is like fine breadcrumbs. Stir in the sugar. Beat the syrup and egg together. Warm the milk and stir in the soda. Add to the egg mixture, beat well and pour into the dry ingredients. Beat well. Put into the prepared tin. Bake for 1 hour 10 minutes. Leave in the tin for 10 minutes, then turn on to a wire rack to cool.

Grasmere Gingerbread

6 oz (150 g) wholemeal flour
2 oz (50 g) porridge oats
2 tsp ground ginger
1 tsp cream of tartar
½ tsp bicarbonate of soda
6 oz (150 g) butter
6 oz (150 g) dark soft brown sugar
2 oz (50 g) chopped mixed candied peel

Grease a 7 × 11 in. (17.5 × 27.5 cm) tin. Preheat oven to 325°F/160°C/Gas Mark 3. Stir together the flour, oats, ginger, cream of tartar and soda. Rub in the butter until the mixture is like fine breadcrumbs. Stir in the sugar and peel. Press into the tin with a fork. Bake for 30 minutes. Leave in the tin for 5 minutes and mark into fingers. Leave in the tin until cold and lift out carefully.

Grantham Gingerbreads

Grantham was once an important staging post on the Great North Road and in the early eighteenth century travellers sustained themselves with Grantham Whetstones – solid, heavy biscuits. In 1740 William Egglestone was working in his shuttered baker's shop and somehow included a raising agent in his biscuits so that they doubled in size. These light, almost hollow ginger biscuits became very popular instead of the 'whetstones'.

8 oz (225 g) self-raising flour
1 tsp ground ginger
3 oz (75 g) butter
8 oz (225 g) caster sugar
1 egg

Grease two baking sheets. Preheat oven to 300°F/150°C/Gas Mark 2. Sieve the flour and ginger. Cream the butter until light and fluffy and then work in the sugar and the egg. Add the dry ingredients and knead to a dry stiff dough, but do not add any liquid. Take a piece of dough the size of a walnut and roll into a ball with the hands. Continue with the remaining dough. Arrange on the baking sheets, leaving room to spread as the gingerbreads will be about 3 in. (7.5 cm) in diameter when cooked. Bake for 45 minutes. The gingerbreads will look very pale. Leave to cool and harden on the baking sheets before lifting off.

Scots' Ginger Cake

The addition of sultanas and peel and ginger pieces to this cake gives it a welcome juiciness, and makes it filling and nourishing for a lunchbox or picnic.

12 oz (350 g) plain flour
3 tsp ground ginger
1 tsp bicarbonate of soda
¼ tsp salt
6 oz (150 g) butter
3 oz (75 g) dark soft brown sugar
12 tbsp black treacle
3 eggs
5 tbsp milk
4 oz (100 g) chopped mixed candied peel
2 oz (50 g) sultanas
1½ oz (40 g) preserved ginger

Grease and line a 7 in. (17.5 cm) square tin. Preheat oven to 325°F/160°C/Gas Mark 3. Sieve together the flour, ginger, soda and salt. Cream the butter and sugar until light and fluffy and work in the treacle until completely incorporated. Beat the eggs and milk together. Add to the butter alternately with the flour until the mixture is smooth and evenly coloured. Stir in the peel and sultanas. Drain any syrup from the ginger and chop the ginger in small pieces. Stir into the cake mixture. Put into the tin and bake for 1 hour 45 minutes. Leave in the tin for 10 minutes before turning out and cooling on a wire rack.

Ginger Loaf

This is a special treat for those who enjoy the flavour of preserved ginger, which may be crystallized or in syrup. The loaf may be eaten plain, or sliced and spread with butter.

4 oz (100 g) butter
4 oz (100 g) dark soft brown sugar
2 eggs
1½ tbsp black treacle
8 oz (225 g) plain flour
½ tsp baking powder
½ tsp ground ginger
4 oz (100 g) preserved ginger

Grease and base-line a 1 lb (450 g) loaf tin. Preheat oven to 375°F/190°C/Gas Mark 5. Cream the butter and sugar until light and fluffy. Beat the eggs with the treacle. Sieve the flour, baking powder and ginger. Add the eggs and flour alternately to the creamed mixture, beating well between each addition. If using ginger in syrup, drain well and rinse under hot water before chopping the ginger into small pieces (crystallised ginger may be simply chopped). Fold the ginger into the mixture. Place in the prepared tin. Bake for 1¼ hours. Leave in tin for 5 minutes, then turn on to a wire rack to cool.

Ashbourne Gingerbread

This version of gingerbread consists of little short biscuits flavoured with ginger which are surprisingly tempting. They should remain pale when baked.

6 oz (150 g) butter
6 oz (150 g) caster sugar
8 oz (225 g) plain flour
2 tsp ground ginger

Grease two baking sheets. Preheat oven to 300°F/150°C/Gas Mark 2. Cream the butter and sugar until light and fluffy. Sieve the flour and ginger. Work into the creamed mixture to form a smooth dough. Take a teaspoonful of the mixture, roll into a ball and then into a cylinder. Place on baking sheet and flatten with a palette knife. Repeat until all the mixture is used. Bake for 20 minutes. Lift on to a wire rack to cool.

Golden Syrup Cake

2 oz (50 g) caster sugar
2 oz (50 g) margarine
4 oz (100 g) golden syrup
1 egg
2 tbsp milk
4 oz (100 g) self-raising flour

Grease and base-line an 8 in. (20 cm) sponge sandwich tin. Preheat oven to 375°F/190°C/Gas Mark 5. Put the sugar, margarine and syrup into a pan and heat gently until melted. Cool for 5 minutes. Beat the egg and milk together and beat into the syrup mixture. Sieve the flour into a bowl. Pour in the syrup mixture, beating well until smooth. Spoon into the tin. Bake for 25 minutes. Turn out on to a wire rack to cool. This may be eaten as a plain cake. If preferred, double the mixture and sandwich the two cakes together with ginger marmalade or chunky marmalade, and finish with lemon water icing on top.

Sponge Parkin

A light version of ginger cake which is good plain, but better still if sandwiched with orange or ginger marmalade.

8 oz (225 g) plain flour
1 oz (25 g) baking powder
1 tsp ground ginger
2 oz (50 g) mixed butter and lard
4 oz (100 g) golden syrup
1½ oz (40 g) granulated sugar
2 tbsp milk

Grease two 7 in. (17.5 cm) round sponge tins. Preheat oven to 325°F/160°C/Gas Mark 3. Sieve the flour, baking powder and ginger into a bowl. Put the fat, syrup and sugar into a pan and heat until melted. Stir in the milk and add to the dry ingredients. Beat well and pour into sponge tins. Bake for 45 minutes. Cool on a wire rack and sandwich together with marmalade.

Schoolboy's Ginger Cake

This is typical of the 'good plain' or 'nursery' cakes which appeared so often in Victorian and turn-of-the-century cookery books. These descriptions were applied to quickly made inexpensive cakes which were considered nourishing for the young without being too exciting for their digestions.

8 oz (225 g) self-raising flour
½ tsp ground ginger
4 oz (100 g) light soft brown sugar
2 oz (50 g) lard
2 oz (50 g) margarine
3 oz (75 g) black treacle
1 oz (25 g) chopped mixed candied peel
1 egg
5 tbsp milk

Grease and line a 1½ lb (675 g) loaf tin. Preheat oven to 350°F/180°C/Gas Mark 4. Stir together the flour, ginger and sugar. Rub in the fat until the mixture is like fine breadcrumbs. Warm the treacle until just runny and add to the dry ingredients. Stir in the peel. Beat the egg and milk together and beat into the mixture. Put in the tin and bake for 1¼ hours. Leave in the tin for 5 minutes, then turn out on to a wire rack to cool.

Parlies

This type of gingerbread comes from Scotland and was supposed to be eaten by members of the Scottish Parliament, hence the name of Parliament Cakes or Parlies. The recipe came from Mrs Fletcher who provided ginger cakes for the schoolboys of Edinburgh when Sir Walter Scott was a boy. There were the thin crisp Parliament Cakes cut in squares, round Snaps, and White or Brown Quality Cakes, probably similar to the Grantham Gingerbreads.

8 oz (225 g) plain flour
4 oz (100 g) dark soft brown sugar
1 oz (25 g) ground ginger
4 oz (100 g) unsalted butter
4 oz (100 g) black treacle

Grease a baking sheet. Preheat oven to 300°F/150°C/Gas Mark 2. Stir the flour, sugar and ginger together in a bowl. Melt the butter and treacle together and bring to the boil. Pour on to the dry ingredients and work together to make a smooth dough. Roll out the dough to fit the baking sheet. Bake for 30 minutes. Remove from oven and mark into squares. Leave in the tin until cold and then separate into pieces.

6 *Fruit Cakes and Fruit Loaves*

And see! what a mountainous bride-cake! – a thing
By itself – with small pieces to pass through a ring!
(R. Barham, *Ingoldsby Legends*)

Dried fruit has been one of the most popular British foods since Roman times, and travellers have often commented in print on our fondness for well-fruited cakes and puddings. Figs and raisins were introduced by the Romans to be eaten as sweetmeats, or to form part of sauces and stuffings. The fruit remained immensely popular with the rich, but could only be indulged in by the poor at festival times, when the fruit provided the essential sweetener for pottages and puddings. From the thirteenth century huge cargoes of figs, prunes, dates, raisins and currants were brought from Southern Europe in the great spice ships. The fruit was still a luxury sweetmeat for the rich, but was also essential food in Lent when it was mixed with bread and made into a meatless pottage called 'figgey' or a sweet sauce called 'rapey' to be served with fried fish. The combination of savoury and sweet mixtures was extremely popular, with dried fruit mixed with fish, and white meat in spiced pies, often containing wine and brandy.

In Tudor times dried fruit was much cheaper than sugar and accordingly used to sweeten many dishes. Currants in particular were very popular, and when it was suggested that Greece might reduce her export of currants there were stories that those who could not afford to buy the scarce food for high-days and holy-days hung themselves. Currants were so-called as they were 'raisins of Corinth' to distinguish them from the larger 'raisins of the sun' and Corinth became corrupted to 'currant'.

The early fruit pottages of medieval times developed into puddings, mincemeat and cakes, but perhaps the earliest example of the fruit cake was the fourteenth-century spitted batter. Dried fruit was impaled on a spit and as the iron rod revolved in front of a hot fire, batter was dripped over the hot fruit and gradually built up into a crisp fruit-filled confection which was eaten hot (similar spit-batters are still available in Germany).

The first true fruit cakes were enriched breads wrapped around fruit, such as Lardy Cake (p. 47), or with the fruit incorporated in the dough, along with candied citrus fruits and nuts. Some of these cakes became very rich indeed, as recorded by Mary Kettilby (*A Collection of Receipts*, second edition 1719) in her appropriately named 'Extraordinary Plumb-Cake':

> Take seven pound of fine Flower, and two pound and half of Butter; put the Butter into the Flower; seven pound of Currants, and two large nutmegs, with half an ounce of Mace, and a quarter of an ounce of Cloves, all finely beat and grated; one pound of sugar,

sixteen Eggs, leaving out four whites, put in a full pint and half of Ale-yeast; warm as much Cream as you think will wet it, and pour Sack to your Cream, to make it as thick as Batter; beat also one pound of Almonds, with Sack and Orange-flower-Water; but don't let them be fine, but grosly beat; put in a pound of Candy'd Orange, Lemon and Citron-peel, or more, if you desire it very rich; mix all and put into your Hoop with a Paste under it to save the bottom. This was given by one of the nicest House-wives in England; and is as good as ever was made.

This cake was finally iced with a mixture of whipped egg whites and double-refined sugar, orange flower water and 'ambergreese'.

These giant cakes became very popular as the housewife gradually changed from preparing her griddle cakes to oven-baking. The large cakes which were still so similar to bread were baked in the bread oven and originally had to be shaped in circles or ovals freehand like loaves, or placed in earthenware pans. The tin hoop had no base and was placed on paper on a tin sheet, but it helped to keep the cake in shape. While some of the early cakes had contained as much as 14 lb (6.5 kg) flour and the mixture had to be worked for two or three hours, the cakes began to diminish in size to contain around 7 lb (3.25 kg) flour, but even in the late eighteenth century a 'little plum cake' still needed 2 lb (900 kg) flour and 1 lb (450 g) currants. There were 'little', 'plain' or 'common' plum cakes, but they all had the common use of the word 'plum' or 'plumb' which some authorities think derived from the use of prunes, while others feel that it indicated the weight and darkness of the cake.

Many of the early fruit mixtures were enclosed in pastry, giving rise to such confections as the Banbury Cake, the Black Bun and the early Simnel Cakes (see Index) as the pastry acted as a case to give shape to rich fruited mixtures. As the use of eggs as a raising agent increased in the eighteenth century, lighter fruit cakes developed, often supporting one type of fruit such as currants and sultanas. The Victorians were particularly fond of currants, importing twice as many as we do now. The nineteenth-century cake fancier still enjoyed the rich plum cakes, but these became more often associated with such ceremonies as weddings, and the plainer Luncheon Cake was more fashionable for everyday use, often being eaten for a light breakfast with tea or chocolate, for a simple lunch with a glass of wine or sherry, or as the final course of a meal.

Picnic Cake

4 oz (100 g) butter
8 oz (225 g) caster sugar
3 eggs
6 oz (150 g) plain flour
½ tsp baking powder
¼ tsp salt
½ tsp ground nutmeg
2 tbsp milk
2 tbsp honey
¼ tsp bicarbonate of soda
8 oz (225 g) walnut kernels
1 lb (450 g) seedless raisins

Grease and flour a 2 lb (900 g) loaf tin. Preheat the oven to 325°F/160°C/Gas Mark 3. Cream the butter and sugar until light and fluffy. Beat the eggs together. Sieve the flour with the baking powder, salt and nutmeg. Add the eggs to the creamed mixture in small quantities alternately with the flour mixture. Stir together the milk, honey and soda and add to the mixture. Reserve 8 walnut halves and chop the rest roughly. Add chopped nuts and raisins to the cake mixture. Spoon into the loaf tin. Bake for 1½ hours and then place reserved walnuts on top. Continue baking for 45 minutes. Cool in tin for 30 minutes, and then turn out on a wire rack to cool.

Fruit Spice Cake

1½ lb (675 g) seedless raisins
4 oz (100 g) chopped mixed candied peel
4 oz (100 g) chopped walnuts
10 oz (300 g) plain flour
1 tsp bicarbonate of soda
¾ tsp ground cinnamon
¾ tsp ground nutmeg
¾ tsp ground cloves
¼ tsp ground ginger
8 oz (225 g) butter
7 oz (175 g) caster sugar
4 eggs
6 tbsp black treacle
6 tbsp cold black coffee

Grease and line a 9 in. (22.5 cm) round cake tin. Preheat oven to 300°F/150°C/Gas Mark 2. Mix the raisins, peel and walnuts together. Sieve the flour, soda and spices together. Cream the butter and sugar together until light and fluffy. Mix the eggs, treacle and coffee. Add to the creamed mixture alternately with the flour. Stir in the fruit and nuts. Mix well and spoon into tin. Bake for 2½ hours. Leave in the tin for 1 hour, then turn out on a wire rack to cool.

Old-Fashioned Plum Cake

12 oz (350 g) self-raising flour
¼ tsp salt
¼ tsp ground nutmeg
4 oz (100 g) butter
6 oz (150 g) currants
3 oz (75 g) sultanas
3 oz (75 g) stoned raisins
2 oz (50 g) glacé cherries
2 oz (50 g) chopped mixed candied peel
6 oz (150 g) granulated sugar
½ pt (300 ml) milk
1 oz (25 g) fresh yeast *or* ½ oz (15 g) dried yeast

Grease and line a 2 lb (900 g) loaf tin. Preheat oven to 300°F/150°C/ Gas Mark 2. Sieve the flour, salt and nutmeg into a bowl and rub in the butter until the mixture is like coarse crumbs. Stir in the currants, sultanas, and raisins. Chop the cherries and add to the mixture with the peel. Stir in the sugar, keeping 1 teaspoonful. Warm the milk to lukewarm. Cream the fresh yeast with the remaining sugar and add to the warm milk, leaving for 5 minutes until bubbling. If using dried yeast, sprinkle on the surface of the milk and leave for 15–20 minutes until frothing and bubbly. Make a well in the centre of the dry ingredients and pour in the milk. Beat well until thoroughly mixed and pour into the tin. Bake for 2¼ hours, covering with a piece of greaseproof paper after the first hour. Turn out on a wire rack to cool. Keep in a tin for a couple of days and eat plain or sliced and buttered.

Raisin Cake

It is important to use nice plump sticky raisins for this cake. It is rather a nuisance to remove the seeds but sometimes they are sold ready-seeded. They are not at all the same as 'seedless raisins' but have a much richer flavour. The cake may be made with butter or with dripping in the old-fashioned way.

1 lb (450 g) plain flour
2 tsp baking powder
6 oz (150 g) butter *or* dripping
8 oz (225 g) granulated sugar
Grated rind of ½ lemon
12 oz (350 g) seeded raisins
2 eggs
7½ fl oz (225 ml) milk

Grease and line an 8 in. (20 cm) round cake tin. Sieve the flour and baking powder into a basin and rub in the fat until the mixture is like fine breadcrumbs. Stir in the sugar and lemon rind and then the raisins. Beat the eggs and milk together and work into the mixture which should be fairly stiff. Put into tin and bake for 1½ hours. Leave in tin for 5 minutes, then turn on to a wire rack to cool.

Shilling Cake

The ingredients for this cake cost 1/– (5p) in 1910.

8 oz (225 g) plain flour
¼ tsp bicarbonate of soda
Grated rind of ½ lemon
4 oz (100 g) butter
6 oz (150 g) seedless raisins
4 oz (100 g) granulated sugar
1 egg
Milk

Grease and line a 6 in. (15 cm) cake tin. Preheat oven to 325°F/160°C/Gas Mark 3. Sieve the flour and soda. Stir in the lemon rind and rub in the butter until the mixture is like coarse crumbs. Stir in the raisins and sugar. Beat the egg lightly and stir into the mixture with enough milk to make a soft dropping consistency. Spoon into the tin. Bake for 1¾ hours. Leave in the tin for 30 minutes, then turn out on a wire rack to cool.

Date and Seed Cake

12 oz (350 g) self-raising flour
6 oz (150 g) caster sugar
5 oz (125 g) dripping
4 oz (100 g) stoned block dates
1 tbsp caraway seeds
1 egg
1 tsp vinegar
Milk

Grease and line a 7 in. (17.5 cm) round cake tin. Preheat oven to 325°F/160°C/Gas Mark 3. Sieve the flour. Cream the sugar and dripping until soft and light. Fold in the flour, chopped dates and caraway seeds. Add the beaten egg. Add the vinegar and the milk and mix to a soft dropping consistency. Spoon into the tin. Bake for 1½ hours. Leave in the tin for 30 minutes, then turn out on a wire rack to cool.

Prune Cake

5 oz (125 g) butter
5 oz (125 g) caster sugar
Grated rind of 1 lemon
2 eggs
6 oz (150 g) prunes
8 oz (225 g) plain flour
1 tsp baking powder

Grease and line a 7 in. (17.5 cm) round cake tin. Preheat oven to 325°F/160°C/Gas Mark 3. Cream the butter and sugar until light and fluffy and work in the lemon rind. Beat the eggs and add to the mixture a little at a time, beating well between each addition. Chop the prunes finely. Sieve the flour and baking powder. Add the prunes and flour to the creamed mixture, with a little milk if necessary, to make a soft dropping consistency. Spoon into the tin. Bake for 1½ hours. Leave in the tin for 30 minutes, then turn out on a wire rack to cool.

School Cake

The tuck box has always been an important part of school life. Public schools flourished and multiplied in the nineteenth century, and many former grammar schools began to take boarding pupils and achieved a higher status. Most professional families and prosperous farmers sent their sons away to school accompanied by boxes of food to offset the horrors of school meals and to fill ever-hungry growing children. Tins of sardines, biscuits and solid fruit cakes were particularly popular, and remain so today.

12 oz (350 g) wholemeal flour
8 oz (225 g) plain flour
2 tsp baking powder
1 tsp ground mixed spice
4 oz (100 g) butter
4 oz (100 g) lard or dripping
8 oz (225 g) granulated sugar
1 lb (450 g) seedless raisins
8 oz (225 g) currants
4 oz (100 g) chopped mixed candied peel
2 eggs
¼ pt (150 ml) milk

Grease and line a 10 in. (25 cm) round cake tin. Preheat oven to 350°F/180°C/Gas Mark 4. Stir together the wholemeal and plain flours, baking powder and spice in a basin. Rub in the fats until the mixture is like fine breadcrumbs. Stir in the sugar and fruit. Beat the eggs and milk together and work into the flour mixture. The mixture should be stiff, but a little more milk may be added to give the right consistency. Put into tin and bake for 2 hours, covering the cake with a piece of greaseproof paper for the last 30 minutes if the cake is getting too brown. Leave in tin for 5 minutes then turn on to a wire rack to cool.

Tray Fruit Cake

10 oz (300 g) self-raising flour
2 tsp ground mixed spice
1 tsp salt
5 oz (125 g) butter
5 oz (125 g) light soft brown sugar
2 eggs
4 tbsp milk
1 lb (450 g) mixed dried fruit

Grease and line a 7 × 11 in. (17.5 × 27.5 cm) rectangular cake tin. Preheat oven to 350°F/180°C/Gas Mark 4. Sieve the flour, spice and salt together and rub in the butter, until the mixture is like coarse crumbs. Stir in the sugar. Beat the eggs and milk together and beat into the mixture. Stir in the fruit and mix well. Spoon into the tin. Bake for 1 hour. Cool in the tin and cut into squares.

Balmoral Cake

This delicious currant cake is for those addicted to almond paste which forms a baked icing. From the same early twentieth-century cookery book comes 'a Plain Balmoral Cake' which omits the currants and the almond paste, which one imagines would not have been so welcome at the royal tea-table.

Cake
8 oz (225 g) butter
8 oz (225 g) caster sugar
3 eggs
8 oz (225 g) plain flour
2 oz (50 g) ground rice
1 tsp baking powder
½ tsp ground cinnamon
12 oz (350 g) currants

Almond paste
3 oz (75 g) ground almonds
3 oz (75 g) caster sugar
Few drops almond essence
1 egg

Decoration
3 oz (75 g) blanched almonds
2 oz (50 g) glacé cherries

Grease and line an 8 in. (20 cm) round cake tin. Preheat oven to 325°F/160°C/Gas Mark 3. Cream the butter and sugar until light and fluffy. Beat the eggs lightly together. Sieve the flour and stir in the rice, baking powder and cinnamon. Add the eggs and flour alternately to the creamed mixture until incorporated. Stir in the currants. Put into the tin and bake for 2½ hours. Cool on a wire rack.

For the paste stir together the ground almonds, caster sugar and almond essence. Beat the egg and add most of it to the mixture, retaining a little for glazing. Shape the almond paste to fit the top of the cake and place on top. Arrange split almonds and cherries around the edge of the cake. Put a cherry in the centre and arrange more almonds to form a star. Brush with egg. Bake for 5 minutes.

Celebration Cake

This rich fruit cake is suitable for Christmas or for weddings or christenings when iced, but it also makes an excellent cake for an ordinary teatime or a rather special picnic. It is sometimes known as Keeping Cake since it will keep in a tin for six months.

8 oz (225 g) butter
8 oz (225 g) soft brown sugar
1 tbsp black treacle
4 large eggs
4 tbsp sherry *or* cold tea
Grated rind of 1 lemon
½ tsp vanilla essence
4 oz (100 g) self-raising flour
6 oz (150 g) plain flour
1 tsp ground mixed spice
¼ tsp salt
Pinch of ground cinnamon
Pinch of ground nutmeg
12 oz (350 g) currants
12 oz (350 g) sultanas
8 oz (225 g) seedless raisins
2 oz (50 g) chopped mixed candied peel
2 oz (50 g) glacé cherries

Grease and line a 10 in. (25 cm) round cake tin. Preheat oven to 300°F/150°C/Gas Mark 2. Cream the butter and sugar with a wooden spoon until light and fluffy. Put the treacle, eggs, sherry or tea, lemon rind and vanilla essence into another bowl. Work them together with a fork just enough to break up the eggs. Sift the flours, spices and salt together. Stir a little of the egg mixture into the butter alternately with the flour mixture, but do not beat. Continue adding liquid and flour until they are all used up. Stir in the fruit and mix just enough to distribute evenly. Put the cake mixture into the tin and level the top with a spoon. Leave to stand for one hour. Bake for 4½ hours. If the top of the cake is becoming very brown halfway through cooking, cover with a double layer of greaseproof paper. Leave in the tin for 45 minutes until lukewarm and turn on to a wire rack to finish cooling. Store in a tin.

Bury Simnel Cake

This version of a Simnel Cake from Bury in Lancashire is probably nearer to the original cake than today's marzipan layered version. It should be about the size of a large teacake and is like a fruit bread in flavour and texture.

8 oz (225 g) plain flour
1 tsp baking powder
¼ tsp ground cinnamon
¼ tsp ground nutmeg
Pinch of salt
4½ oz (115 g) butter
4 oz (100 g) granulated sugar
5 oz (125 g) currants
4 oz (100 g) sultanas
1 oz (25 g) chopped mixed candied peel
2 eggs
2 tbsp milk
1 tbsp golden syrup
Sliced citron peel
Split blanched almonds

Grease a baking sheet. Preheat oven to 450°F/200°C/Gas Mark 6. Sieve together the flour, baking powder, cinnamon and salt. Rub in the butter until the mixture is like fine breadcrumbs. Stir in the sugar, dried fruit and peel. Beat the eggs lightly and reserve 1 tablespoonful. Mix the remaining eggs and milk into the flour to give a firm dough. Form into two round flat cakes about 5 in. (12.5 cm) across and place on the baking sheet. Mix the remaining egg and syrup and brush the surface of the cakes. Decorate one with split almonds and the other with sliced citron peel. Bake for 25 minutes and cool on a wire rack.

Simnel Cake

The name of this cake is derived from *simnellus* (Latin for fine flour) and this particular version is said to come from the area around Shrewsbury. Traditionally it was the cake which was made with figs which represented 'fruitfulness in offspring'. Figs played an important part in pre-Easter days – special fig cakes were often made for Palm Sunday. The Simnel Cake was taken home by servant girls on the fourth Sunday in Lent, known as Mothering Sunday, which was one of the few days in the year when they were allowed to visit their families. Now the cake is more often eaten as an Easter cake. The almond paste balls on top represent the Disciples, without Judas.

8 oz (225 g) butter
8 oz (225 g) sugar
12 oz (350 g) plain flour
2 tsp baking powder
4 oz (100 g) chopped mixed candied peel
2 tbsp milk
1 lb (450 g) almond paste

1 tsp ground cinnamon
Pinch of ground nutmeg
4 eggs
1½ lb (700 g) mixed dried fruit
2 tbsp sieved jam
1 tbsp egg white
1 tbsp caster sugar
4 tbsp glacé icing

Grease an 8 in. (20 cm) round cake tin. Preheat oven to 325°F/160°C/Gas Mark 3. Cream the butter and sugar with a wooden spoon until light and fluffy. Sift together the flour, baking powder, cinnamon and nutmeg. Beat the eggs until just mixed. Add the eggs gradually to the creamed mixture alternately with a little of the flour. When thoroughly mixed, add the remaining flour, dried fruit and peel. Add a little milk if necessary, but the cake mixture should be stiff. Roll out the almond paste into two 8 in. (20 cm) rounds, and reserve all the trimmings. Put half the cake mixture into the tin and cover with one round of almond paste. Press down very lightly so that the almond paste fits firmly on the cake mixture. Put in the remaining cake mixture. Bake for 3 hours. Cool in the tin. When cold, turn out and place on a cake board. Brush the top with jam and place the second round of almond paste on top. Roll the almond paste trimmings into eleven small balls and arrange in a circle on the cake. Flatten them slightly with the hands. Brush the surface of the almond paste with egg white and sprinkle with caster sugar. Put under a hot grill until the sugar has coloured to a light beige and given the almond paste a slightly crystalline surface. When cold, put a circle of glacé icing in the centre of the cake. If liked, the cake may be decorated with sugar eggs and fluffy chickens, and a white or yellow satin ribbon may be tied around the circumference.

Dundee Cake

Nobody seems to know why this deliciously light and crumbly fruit cake should come from Dundee, but there is a story that it is a by-product of the marmalade industry and that the orange flavour was originally introduced by using marmalade in the cake rather than the now traditional candied peel and citrus fruit rinds.

8 oz (225 g) butter
8 oz (225 g) caster sugar
5 eggs
8 oz (225 g) self-raising flour
½ tsp ground nutmeg
3 oz (75 g) glacé cherries
Grated rind of 1 orange
Grated rind of 1 lemon
6 oz (150 g) currants
6 oz (150 g) sultanas
2 oz (50 g) chopped mixed candied peel
3 oz (75 g) ground almonds
2 oz (50 g) whole blanched almonds

Grease a 10 in. (25 cm) round cake tin. Preheat the oven to 325°F/160°C/Gas Mark 3. Cream the butter and sugar together with a wooden spoon until light and fluffy. Add the eggs one at a time with a teaspoon of flour and beat well after each addition. Sift the remaining flour with the nutmeg and fold into the creamed mixture. Rinse and dry the cherries and cut them in quarters. Fold in the orange and lemon rinds, currants, sultanas, cherries and peel and mix well. Finally, fold in the ground almonds. Put the cake mixture into the tin and slightly hollow the centre with the back of a tablespoon. Bake for 1½ hours. Very gently draw the cake part-way out of the oven, and quickly arrange the almonds on the top in circles. Put them on the cake very lightly. Return the cake to the oven and continue baking for 1 hour. Leave to cool in the tin for 10 minutes, and then turn on to a wire rack to finish cooling.

Black Bun

'Bun' is an old Scots word for rich fruit cake and Black Bun is a very rich cake made for the Hogmanay (New Year's Eve) celebrations. It was formerly eaten at Twelfth Night parties, and consists of a filling rather like Christmas pudding inside a strong pastry case. This pastry was formerly discarded when the 'bun' was eaten – this kind of pastry known as 'huff pastry' was often wrapped around such things as ham and venison so that they could be cooked very slowly, rather in the way we use foil nowadays. The pastry was not considered fit for the gentry but was very welcome for servants and beggars since it was soaked with the juices of the food cooked inside. Today, slices of Black Bun, including the pastry, are washed down with the New Year drink 'Het Pint', a hot mixture of spiced ale, eggs and whisky.

Pastry case
1 lb (450 g) plain flour
8 oz (225 g) butter
1 tbsp caster sugar
6 tbsp water
Beaten egg to glaze

Filling
1 lb (450 g) plain flour
2 tsp ground cinnamon
1 tsp ground ginger
1 tsp ground nutmeg
½ tsp ground allspice
Pinch of black pepper
1 tsp salt
1 tsp bicarbonate of soda
6 oz (150 g) dark soft brown sugar
2 lb (900 g) currants
2 lb (900 g) stoned raisins
8 oz (225 g) chopped mixed candied peel
8 oz (225 g) chopped blanched almonds
2 tbsp brandy
¼ pt (150 ml) milk

Grease and lightly flour a 10 in. (25 cm) round cake tin. Preheat oven to 325°F/160°C/Gas Mark 3. Make the pastry case first. Rub the butter into the flour until the mixture is like fine breadcrumbs. Stir in the sugar and add the water to make a firm dough. Roll out on a floured board and cut off two-thirds of the pastry. Line the cake tin with the larger piece of pastry. Roll the remaining pastry into a circle for a lid.

To make the filling, sieve the flour with the spices, salt and bicarbonate of soda. Mix with the sugar, dried fruit, peel and almonds Add the brandy and milk to make a very stiff mixture. Spoon into th pastry case and flatten the top with the back of a spoon. Dampen the top of the pastry with a little water and put on the pastry lid. Pinch the edges together to seal them firmly. Prick all over the lid with a fork. Take a skewer and make three holes from the top right down to the base of the cake. Brush the lid with beaten egg. Bake for 3 hours. Cool in the tin. The cake should be made about two months before it is needed so that the flavourings mature.

Scripture Cake

This cake was a great favourite in mid-Victorian times, and I suspect that small children were set to look up the Biblical references before they were allowed to taste the results of their labours. Quantities vary in different manuscripts and books, but the references remain the same.

4½ cups I Kings Chapter 3 Verse 22 (flour)
1½ cups Judges 5 v. 25 (butter)
2 cups Jeremiah 6 v. 20 (sugar)
2 cups I Samuel 30 v. 12 (raisins)
2 cups Nahum 3 v. 12 (figs)
1 cup Numbers 17 v. 8 (almonds)
2 tablespoons I Samuel 14 v. 25 (honey)
Season to taste II Chronicles 9 v. 9 (spice)
6 articles Jeremiah 17 v. 11 (eggs)
1 pinch Leviticus 11 v. 13 (salt)
1 cup Judges 4 v. 19 last clause (milk)
3 teaspoons Amos 5 v. 5 (yeast)

Follow Solomon's prescription for the making of a good boy Proverbs 23 v. 14 (beat it well).

Those who would like to try the recipe may try my modern version which produces a spiced luncheon cake. A few years ago we sold the recipe for church funds and made a lot of money, and we also made up the mixture into small 'cup cakes' in paper cases which sold by the hundred and further added to the funds.

6 oz (150 g) butter *or* soft margarine
8 oz (225 g) caster sugar
3 eggs
12 oz (350 g) plain flour
1½ tsp baking powder
1 tsp ground mixed spice
Pinch of salt
1 tbsp honey
¼ pt (150 ml) milk
12 oz (350 g) mixed dried fruit
1½ oz (40 g) almonds

Grease and base-line an 8 in. (20 cm) round cake tin. Preheat oven to 350°F/180°C/Gas Mark 4. Cream the fat and sugar until light and fluffy. Beat the eggs lightly. Sieve together the flour, baking powder, spice and salt. Add eggs and flour alternately to the creamed mixture, beating well between each addition. Beat in the honey and milk. Stir in fruit and chopped almonds. Put into the prepared tin. Bake for 1½ hours, covering cake if it becomes too brown. Leave in tin for 10 minutes, then turn on to a wire rack to cool.

Irish Porter Cake

This Irish fruit cake is moistened with Guinness, first brewed in 1759 in Dublin, as a version of porter, a kind of weak stout which was widely used in the British Isles for cooking as well as drinking. A similar cake from the West Country is known as Penzance Cake.

8 oz (225 g) butter
8 oz (225 g) dark soft brown sugar
4 eggs
10 oz (300 g) plain flour
2 tsp ground mixed spice
8 oz (225 g) seedless raisins
8 oz (225 g) sultanas
4 oz (100 g) chopped mixed candied peel
4 oz (100 g) chopped walnut halves
8 tbsp Guinness

Grease and line a 7 in. (17.5 cm) round cake tin. Preheat oven to 325°F/160°C/Gas Mark 3. Cream the butter and sugar with a wooden spoon until light and fluffy. Break the eggs into another bowl and beat them lightly until they are just mixed. Gradually add to the creamed mixture, beating well. Sieve together the flour and spice. Gradually fold into the creamed mixture. Add the raisins, sultanas, peel and nuts and mix well together. Stir in half the Guinness to give a soft mixture which will drop easily from a spoon. Put the mixture into the tin. Bake for 1 hour. Reduce heat to 300°F/150°C/Gas Mark 2 and continue cooking the cake for 1½ hours. Leave in the tin until cold. Turn out on to a wire rack, base upwards. Prick the base of the cake in eight places with a skewer to the depth of 1 in. (2.5 cm). Spoon over the remaining Guinness. Leave to stand for 40 minutes. Wrap in a piece of greaseproof paper and store in a tin for 1 week before eating.

Bara Brith

Often known as Speckled Bread this is a favourite Welsh recipe which is rich and moist and very easy to make. There are many variations, with and without yeast, but the cake is traditionally served sliced with butter.

1 lb (450 g) mixed dried fruit
8 oz (225 g) demerara sugar
Warm tea (without milk)
2 rounded tbsp marmalade
1½ tsp ground cinnamon
1 egg
1 lb (450 g) self-raising flour

Put the fruit into a bowl with the sugar and just cover with warm strained tea. Leave overnight. Grease and base-line a 2 lb (900 g) loaf tin. Preheat oven to 325°F/160°C/Gas Mark 3. Stir the marmalade, cinnamon, egg and flour into the fruit mixture and beat well until completely blended. Place in the prepared tin. Bake for 1½ hours. Leave in the tin for 15 minutes, then turn on to a wire rack to cool. Store in a tin for 24 hours before cutting.

Marmalade Fruit Cake

8 oz (225 g) self-raising flour
2 oz (50 g) butter
2 oz (50 g) lard
4 oz (100 g) granulated sugar
4 oz (100 g) mixed dried fruit
1 tsp ground mixed spice
Grated rind of ½ lemon
Pinch of salt
2 tbsp chunky orange marmalade
6 fl oz (150 ml) milk
1 tsp vinegar

Grease and line a 2 lb (900 g) loaf tin. Preheat oven to 350°F/180°C/Gas Mark 4. Sieve the flour into a bowl and rub in the butter and lard until the mixture is like coarse crumbs. Stir in the sugar, fruit, spice, lemon rind and salt. Add the marmalade, milk and vinegar and mix well. Spoon the mixture into the tin and level the top lightly. Bake for 1¼ hours. Turn on to a wire rack to cool.

West Country Cream Cake

6 oz (150 g) butter
6 oz (150 g) demerara sugar
3 eggs
8 fl oz (200 ml) double cream
1 tbsp black treacle
4 oz (100 g) stoned raisins
4 oz (100 g) sultanas
4 oz (100 g) currants
12 oz (350 g) self-raising flour
Pinch of salt

Grease and line a 7 in. (17.5 cm) round cake tin. Preheat oven to 325°F/160°C/Gas Mark 3. Cream the butter and sugar until light and fluffy. Add the eggs one at a time, beating well. Warm the cream and treacle together over low heat. Add to the creamed mixture and stir in the fruit. Fold in the flour sifted with the salt. Mix well and spoon into the tin. Bake for 2½ hours. Cool in the tin for 30 minutes and then turn out on a wire rack to cool.

Scratchins Cake

Once upon a time, every cottager kept a pig known as 'the gentleman who pays the rent'. Pork was the only meat known to many country families along with the odd chicken, rabbit, or pheasant, as 'butcher's meat' was considered far too expensive. It was said that every part of the pig except the squeak was used, and this included the rich pig fat. The pieces of fat were cut into pieces and placed in baking tins, then heated gently in a low oven or on top of the stove. The liquid fat was poured off to make lard for cooking or spreading (children never ate butter, but had lard flavoured with rosemary spread on their bread), or for making ointment. The fat was heated until every scrap of liquid fat had been driven off, and a pan of crisp tasty pieces of fat was left. These were eaten sprinkled with salt, or spread on hot toast, and some were left to get cold. These pieces were chopped and either mixed with dried fruit in a pastry tart, or included in a fruit cake.

1 lb (450 g) self-raising flour
8 oz (225 g) scratchins
6 oz (150 g) demerara sugar
8 oz (225 g) stoned raisins
Grated rind of 2 lemons
1 egg
¾ pt (450 ml) sour milk

Grease and line a 9 in. (22.5 cm) round cake tin. Preheat oven to 350°F/180°C/Gas Mark 4. Sieve the flour and stir in the scratchins, sugar, raisins and lemon rind. Beat the egg and milk together and work into the dry ingredients. Beat and put in the prepared tin. Bake for 1½ hours. Leave in tin for 10 minutes, then turn on to a wire rack to cool.

Vinegar Cake

An economical cake made with vinegar has been popular for generations with those who could not afford to use eggs for baking. This kind of recipe has been very useful too when eggs are scarce or unobtainable, as during the Second World War. In effect, the vinegar sours the milk and reacts with the soda to give a light texture.

12 oz (350 g) plain flour
4 oz (100 g) butter or dripping
4 oz (100 g) caster sugar
3 oz (75 g) sultanas
3 oz (75 g) currants
1 oz (25 g) chopped mixed candied peel
½ tsp bicarbonate of soda
12 tbsp milk
1½ tbsp vinegar

Grease and line an 8 in. (25 cm) round cake tin. Preheat oven to 350°F/180°C/Gas Mark 4. Sift the flour into a bowl and rub in the fat until the mixture is like fine breadcrumbs. Stir in the sugar, sultanas, currants and peel. Mix the soda with a little of the milk and then add to the remaining milk. Stir into the dry ingredients and add the vinegar. Mix well and pour into the tin. Bake for 1½ hours. Cool in the tin for 5 minutes, then turn on to a wire rack to cool.

Twelfth Night Cake

Twelfth Day was second only to Christmas Day as an occasion for feasting and merriment. The winter festivities lasted for twelve days but Old Christmas Day was actually celebrated on 6 January before the calendar was changed in the eighteenth century. Today we celebrate Twelfth Night on that day, and have a tradition that all Christmas decorations must be removed from the house (they used to be left in church until Candlemas on 2 February). In older apple districts, Twelfth Night is celebrated with wassailing or singing, and the trees are peppered by shotguns and cider poured on their roots to ensure a good yield in the coming season.

A special cake was prepared for Twelfth Day, and the custom remains in France and at the Drury Lane Theatre in London where it is remade in memory of Robert Baddeley, a cook-turned-actor, who left money in 1794 to provide cake and wine on Twelfth Night for the company currently playing at the theatre. Basically the cake is a richly flavoured fruit cake, sometimes iced, or decorated with a gold paper frill to represent the crowns of the Three Kings at Epiphany also celebrated on 6 January. The most important constituent of the cake is the representation of the king and queen. In France, tiny china models have been used for centuries, but here we use a bean and a pea. The man with the bean is crowned 'king' at midnight, while the woman with the pea becomes 'queen'.

8 oz (225 g) unsalted butter
8 oz (225 g) caster sugar
4 eggs
3 tbsp brandy
8 oz (225 g) plain flour
¼ tsp ground cinnamon
¼ tsp ground nutmeg
8 oz (225 g) currants
8 oz (225 g) seedless raisins
4 oz (100 g) sultanas
3 oz (75 g) blanched almonds
1 dried bean and 1 dried pea

Grease and line a 10 in. (25 cm) round cake tin. Preheat oven to 300°F/150°C/Gas Mark 2. Cream the butter and sugar until light and fluffy. Beat the eggs with brandy. Sieve the flour with spices. Add the eggs and flour alternately to the creamed mixture, beating well between each addition. Stir in the dried fruit. Chop the nuts and fold into the mixture. Put into the prepared tin and press the bean and pea down into the mixture. Bake for 3 hours. Leave in tin for 15 minutes, then turn on to a rack to cool.

Cumberland Buttermilk Cake

1 lb (450 g) plain flour
3 oz (75 g) lard
3 oz (75 g) unsalted butter
4 oz (100 g) caster sugar
8 oz (225 g) chopped candied lemon peel
4 oz (100 g) stoned raisins
2 heaped tbsp marmalade
¼ pt (150 ml) buttermilk *or* sour milk
1 tsp bicarbonate of soda

Grease and line an 8 in. (20 cm) round cake tin. Preheat oven to 325°F/160°C/Gas Mark 3. Sieve the flour and rub in the fats until the mixture is like fine breadcrumbs. Stir in the sugar, peel, raisins and marmalade. Warm the milk to lukewarm, stir in the soda, and add to the cake mixture. Add a little more milk if necessary to make a soft dough. Put into the prepared cake tin. Bake for 1 hour. Reduce heat to 300°F/150°C/Gas Mark 2, and continue baking for 45 minutes. Leave in tin for 10 minutes, then turn on to a wire rack to cool.

Bread Pudding

Although this is officially called 'pudding' it is most commonly eaten as cake. It dates from the days when every bit of bread was precious and had to be recycled in other dishes, but has become an important standby in many cafés and fashionable 'hot bread shops', perhaps for the same reason that it uses up unsold bread. The cake is solid, wet and heavy, but is a popular and sustaining snack with a strong cup of tea. Leftover buns may be included in the mixture, and the pudding may be served hot with custard before being left to get cold as a cake.

8 slices bread (toast thickness)
½ pt (300 ml) milk
12 oz (350 g) mixed dried fruit
2 oz (50 g) chopped mixed candied peel
1 eating apple
3 tbsp dark soft brown sugar
2 heaped tbsp marmalade
3 tbsp self-raising flour
2 eggs
Squeeze of lemon juice
1 tsp ground cinnamon
4 oz (100 g) butter
Icing sugar

Grease a 10 × 14 in. (25 × 35 cm) roasting tin. Preheat oven to 300°F/150°C/Gas Mark 2. Soak the bread, including the crusts, in the milk until soft. Beat in the dried fruit and peel. Peel the apple and grate the flesh into the mixture. Add the sugar, marmalade, flour, eggs, lemon juice and cinnamon. Beat very thoroughly together until the mixture is evenly coloured. Melt the butter and add half to the mixture. Beat well and put into the prepared tin. Pour on the remaining butter. Bake for 1½ hours. Increase heat to 350°F/180°C/Gas Mark 4 and continue baking for 30 minutes. Leave in the tin until cold and sprinkle thickly with sieved icing sugar before cutting into squares.

Irish Whiskey Cake

2 tbsp Irish whiskey
1 orange
6 oz (150 g) sultanas
6 oz (150 g) butter
6 oz (150 g) caster sugar
3 eggs
8 oz (225 g) plain flour
1 tsp baking powder
Pinch of salt

Grease and line a 7 in. (17.5 cm) round cake tin. Preheat oven to 350°F/180°C/Gas Mark 4. Put the whiskey into a small bowl. Peel the orange very thinly and leave the rind to soak in the whiskey with the sultanas. Cream the butter and sugar until light and fluffy. Beat the eggs lightly. Sieve the flour, baking powder and salt. Add the eggs and flour alternately to the creamed mixture, beating well between each addition. Fold in the remaining flour. Remove the orange peel from the whiskey and discard. Stir in the whiskey and sultanas into the cake mixture. Put into the prepared tin. Bake for 1 hour 15 minutes. Leave in tin for 10 minutes, then turn on to a wire rack to cool.

Palm Sunday Fig Cake

The fig is said to represent 'fruitfulness in offspring' and was widely used in celebration cakes and puddings (e.g. the Figgy Pudding at Christmas). In Cornwall 'figgy' indicates the use of raisins, but this recipe does really use the original figs.

6 oz (150 g) dried figs
Water
6 oz (150 g) plain flour
½ tsp baking powder
Pinch of salt
2½ oz (65 g) caster sugar
2½ oz (65 g) butter

Grease and base-line a 7 in. (17.5 cm) round cake tin. Preheat oven to 375°F/190°C/Gas Mark 5. Chop the figs roughly and simmer in just enough water to cover them until they are tender and leave to cool in the liquid. Sieve together the flour, baking powder and salt. Stir in the sugar and rub in the butter until the mixture is well blended. Mix to a batter with the figs and liquid. Put into the prepared tin. Bake for 45 minutes. Leave in tin for 5 minutes, then turn on to a wire rack to cool.

Harvest Betsy Cake

Barley flour was once widely used for British baking, along with oats and rye. Barley and oats were particularly good for griddle-baking, but were not suitable for raising with yeast, and as housewives turned from the griddle to the oven at the end of the eighteenth century, the use of these flours began to die out. Barley flour may be bought at some health food shops, and is worth trying for this early type of harvest cake.

8 oz (225 g) barley flour
8 oz (225 g) plain flour
1½ tsp baking powder
½ tsp salt
4 oz (100 g) caster sugar
4 oz (100 g) butter
2 tsp black treacle
½ pt (300 ml) milk
8 oz (225 g) sultanas

Grease and base-line a 7 in. (17.5 cm) round cake tin. Preheat oven to 325°F/160°C/Gas Mark 3. Sieve the flours together with the baking powder and salt. Cream the sugar and butter until light and fluffy and work in the treacle. Add the flour and milk alternately until incorporated. Fold in the sultanas. Put into the prepared tin. Bake for 1½ hours. Cool in tin for 10 minutes, then turn on to a wire rack to cool.

Luncheon Cake

As early as the fourteenth century 'nunchin' existed as a snack between meals, and by the seventeenth century 'lunch' or 'luncheon' was defined as 'such food as one's hand can hold'. It was considered to be a hurried and slightly vulgar meal for men of business, and might consist of cold meat and sherry, or of coffee and pastries. At that time, breakfast was a mid-morning meal and dinner appeared somewhere between 2 and 4 p.m., and ladies did not find it necessary to fill the gap with food, but preferred to shop, pay visits or see exhibitions in the hours between meals. However, as commercial life became important in the late eighteenth century, men spent longer hours in offices, so that there was a long period between an 8 o'clock breakfast and dinner which was moved to the early evening. Men of leisure used the extra time to play the new games of cricket and football, or to shoot and hunt, and this left womenfolk with a free day. A new light sociable meal was introduced around midday for ladies and for idle men (the divorce courts became increasingly busy at this period).

The luncheon cake developed at the end of the eighteenth century and remained popular until the 1930s. This light fruit cake, which might also contain caraway seeds and peel, was sometimes a mere snack, but was more often served to finish a meal, along with a glass of port or Madeira, and even with a piece of cheese and an apple. It was popular in gentlemen's clubs, perhaps as a relic of the early lunch of coffee and pastries, and many illustrations to nineteenth-century books show countrymen tucking into a large fruitcake alongside a truckle cheese. Lady Clark of Tillypronie collected no less than nine Luncheon Cake recipes in her book (*The Cookery Book of Lady Clark of Tillypronie*, 1909), ranging from one made with yeast to those listed as Rich; Good; Second Best; Small and Very Light; and for Shooters. The following recipe dates from 1928 and is a good example of this delicious cake.

12 oz (350 g) plain flour
4 oz (100 g) rice flour
8 oz (225 g) granulated sugar
1 tsp ground ginger
½ tsp ground mixed spice
½ tsp salt
2 tsp baking powder
3 oz (75 g) lard
3 oz (75 g) butter
8 oz (225 g) seedless raisins
4 oz (100 g) currants
4 oz (100 g) chopped mixed candied peel
3 eggs
6 tbsp milk

Grease and line an 8 in. (20 cm) round cake tin. Preheat oven to 350°F/180°C/Gas Mark 4. Sieve the flour and rice flour into a basin. Stir in the sugar, ginger, spice, salt and baking powder. Rub in the butter and lard until the mixture is like fine breadcrumbs. Stir in the fruit and peel. Separate the eggs and beat the egg yolks and milk together. Mix into the flour mixture until well blended. Whisk the egg whites to stiff peaks and fold into the mixture. Put into the cake tin and bake for 1½ hours. Leave in the tin for 5 minutes, then turn on to a wire rack to cool.

Lady Savill's Plain Luncheon Cake

1 lb (450 g) plain flour
4 oz (100 g) butter
8 oz (225 g) dark soft brown sugar
8 oz (225 g) sultanas
8 oz (225 g) seedless raisins
1 tsp bicarbonate of soda
Pinch of salt
¼ pt (150 ml) milk

Grease and line an 8 in. (20 cm) round cake tin. Preheat oven to 350°F/180°C/Gas Mark 4. Sieve the flour into a bowl. Rub in the butter until the mixture is like fine breadcrumbs. Stir in the sugar, sultanas and raisins. Dissolve the soda and salt in the milk and add to the dry ingredients. Beat well and pour into the tin. Bake for 1½ hours. Leave in tin for 5 minutes, and then turn out on a wire rack to cool. The original recipe recommends using sour milk if available to make a lighter cake.

Blackmore Vale Hunt Cake

A very good version of Luncheon Cake which has been enjoyed by members of the Hunt for the last century.

4 oz (100 g) butter
4 oz (100 g) caster sugar
¼ pt (150 ml) milk
2 tsp black treacle
1 tsp bicarbonate of soda
12 oz (350 g) plain flour
8 oz (225 g) stoned raisins
3 oz (75 g) chopped mixed candied peel

Grease and line a 7 in. (17.5 cm) round cake tin. Preheat oven to 350°F/180°C/Gas Mark 4. Cream the butter and sugar until light and fluffy. Heat the milk to lukewarm and stir in the treacle and soda. Add the liquid and the flour alternately to the creamed mixture until incorporated, beating well with each addition. Stir in the raisins and peel. Put into the tin and bake for 2 hours. Leave in the tin for 5 minutes, then turn on to a wire rack to cool.

Deebank Sultana Cake

A nice version of the Lunch Cake from Scotland, with a hint of orange flavour.

12 oz (350 g) butter
12 oz (350 g) caster sugar
1 heaped tbsp marmalade
6 eggs
1 lb (450 g) plain flour
Pinch of salt
1½ lb (675 g) sultanas

Grease and line a 10 in. (25 cm) round cake tin. Preheat oven to 350°F/160°C/Gas Mark 3. Cream the butter and sugar until light and fluffy and work in the marmalade. Beat the eggs in a bowl. Sieve the flour and salt. Add the eggs and flour alternately to the creamed mixture. Fold in any remaining flour and the fruit. Put into the prepared tin. Bake for 2 hours. Cool in the tin for 10 minutes and turn on to a wire rack to cool. Do not eat until the following day.

Wartime Boiled Cake

The 'boiled fruitcake' became very popular during the Second World War because the method ensured plump fruit and a moist cake. This is a very economical cake, but full of flavour.

½ pt (300 ml) water *or* cold tea
3 oz (75 g) block margarine *or* lard
3 oz (75 g) granulated sugar
3 oz (75 g) mixed dried fruit
10 oz (300 g) plain flour
3 tsp baking powder
Pinch of salt
1 tsp ground mixed spice
1 tsp bicarbonate of soda

Grease and flour an 8 in. (20 cm) round cake tin. Preheat oven to 350°F/180°C/Gas Mark 4. Put the water or tea, fat, sugar and fruit into a pan and heat gently until the fat melts. Boil for 2 minutes and leave to cool until lukewarm. Sieve the flour, baking powder, salt, spice and soda together. Pour in the fruit mixture and beat well. Bake for 1½ hours. Cool in the tin for 5 minutes, then turn on to a wire rack to cool.

Miss Pedelty's Boiled Fruit Cake

This version of a boiled cake is very moist and rich, keeps well and is excellent for packed meals.

5 oz (125 g) butter *or* block margarine
6 tbsp golden syrup
¼ pt (150 ml) milk
4 oz (100 g) chopped block dates
8 oz (225 g) currants
4 oz (100 g) sultanas
8 oz (225 g) stoned *or* seedless raisins
4 oz (100 g) chopped mixed candied peel
8 oz (225 g) self-raising flour
1 tsp ground mixed spice
1 tsp ground nutmeg
Pinch of salt
2 eggs
½ tsp bicarbonate of soda

Grease and line a 10 in. (25 cm) round cake tin. Preheat oven to 325°F/160°C/Gas Mark 3. Put the fat, syrup, milk, dried fruit and peel into a pan and heat gently until the fat has melted. Simmer gently for 5 minutes, stirring once or twice. Leave until cool. Sieve the flour, spices and salt together and make a well in the centre. Break in the eggs, but do not stir. Stir the soda into the fruit mixture and pour on to the dry ingredients. Beat very thoroughly until well mixed. Pour into prepared tin. Bake for 1¾ hours. Leave in the tin for 10 minutes, then turn on to a wire rack to cool.

Gemma's Boiled Cake

A light boiled cake with a hint of orange flavour which is often brought to me as a gift by the friend after whom it is named.

8 oz (225 g) mixed dried fruit
8 fl oz (200 ml) water
8 oz (225 g) granulated sugar
4 oz (100 g) block margarine
1 rounded tbsp orange marmalade
2 eggs
8 oz (225 g) self-raising flour

Grease and line an 8 in. (20 cm) round cake tin. Preheat oven to 300°F/150°C/Gas Mark 2. Put the fruit, water, sugar, margarine and marmalade into a pan and simmer for 25 minutes. Leave until cold. Stir in the eggs and flour and beat thoroughly. Pour into prepared tin. Bake for 1 hour, and then reduce heat to 250°F/130°C/Gas Mark ½. Continue baking for 45 minutes. Cool in the tin for 25 minutes and then turn on to a wire rack to cool.

7 Cut-and-Come-Again Cakes

> The result is that heavenly cut-and-come-again sort of cake which is unknown to the drawing room, but the true food of the nursery gods and of those lower regions where, drawn to an irresistible fragrance, even college-bred policemen may linger – and refresh.
>
> (Lorna Bunyard, *The Epicure's Companion*)

A fruit cake may well be a cut-and-come-again cake, but the true cake which rejoices in that evocative name is a plainer affair which is grander than the bun or loaf and more filling than the effete small cake. Early large cakes were raised by yeast which could support plenty of dried fruit, but the ale yeast had a strong flavour which was not attractive in a plain cake. Mary Kettilby (1719 edition) gave a yeast-raised seed cake which involved a quarter of a peck of 'fine flower' with 1½ lb (675 g) butter, a pint (600 ml) cream, a 'pint of good ale-yeast to half a pint of Sack' and was well flavoured with candied peel, orange water and almonds, and 1½ lb (675 g) 'smooth carraways', so it would appear that a good deal had to be done to flavour the non-fruited yeast-raised seed cake. At this period, however, it was beginning to be realised that eggs could be used to give the lightness to such cakes, and that the yeast could be omitted, and Mary Kettilby also gave a recipe for a Carraway Cake without Yeast which needed twenty eggs to raise 5 lb (2.5 kg) flour and 4 lb (900 g) sugar. Seeds were probably used originally for this type of cake because they were light and could be well-distributed in the mixture while the heavy dried fruit would sink.

During the eighteenth century this more refined type of plain cake made by rubbing-in and creaming methods began to be flavoured with Madeira or almonds, and made the perfect accompaniment to wine or the newly popular tea. Their digestibility was appreciated, and they were considered to be suitable for nursery tea, or to serve as an alternative to bread and butter for a light meal, and were certainly appreciated still in the nineteenth century. Charlotte Brontë in *Jane Eyre* gives us a good indication of the state of the seed cake:

> Having invited Helen and me to approach the table, and placed before each of us a cup of tea with one delicious but thin morsel of toast, she got up, unlocked a drawer, and taking from it a parcel wrapped in paper, disclosed presently to our eyes a good-sized seed-cake.
>
> 'I meant to give each of you some of this to take with you', said she; 'but as there is too little toast, you must have it now', and she proceeded to cut slices with a generous hand.
>
> We feasted that evening as on nectar and ambrosia; and not the

least delight of the entertainment was the smile of gratification with which our hostess regarded us, as we satisfied our famished appetite on the delicate fare she liberally supplied.

These plain cakes served another purpose in the economical household because they were considerably cheaper to make without dried fruit, and also saved the labour of preparing the fruit. Such cakes played a large part in the feeding of servants, many of whose meals consisted of tea or cocoa with bread-and-jam or a piece of plain cake. They became the standard household cakes which could be stored in tins and produced over and over again, and they also became that symbol of hospitality which 'something in the tin' implies. In country households, and below-stairs, in town houses, there was a constant stream of casual visitors and tradesmen who needed refreshment and the 'cut-and-come-again' cake was always available.

Seed Loaf

Seed loaf is particularly good if sliced and toasted before the fire, then buttered thickly.

8 oz (225 g) plain flour
½ tsp baking powder
6 oz (150 g) butter
6 oz (150 g) caster sugar
3 eggs
2 tsp caraway seeds
4 tbsp rum *or* milk

Grease and line a 1½ lb (675 g) loaf tin. Preheat oven to 350°F/180°C/Gas Mark 4. Sieve the flour and baking powder together. Cream the butter and sugar until light and fluffy. Beat the eggs together and add alternately with the flour to the creamed mixture. Beat until light and fluffy and stir in the caraway seeds and rum or milk. Spoon into the tin. Bake for 1½ hours. Turn out on a wire rack to cool.

Marble Cake

This is an attractive cake which shows a 'marbling' effect when cut. It may be finished with glacé icing, but is just as good left plain or dusted with sieved icing sugar.

6 oz (150 g) butter
7 oz (175 g) caster sugar
3 eggs
8 oz (225 g) self-raising flour
3 tbsp cold milk
1 tsp vanilla essence
1 oz (25 g) cocoa powder

Grease and line an 8 in. (20 cm) square cake tin. Preheat oven to 375°F/190°C/Gas Mark 5. Cream the butter and sugar until light and fluffy. Separate the eggs and beat the yolks into the creamed mixture with a little of the flour. Fold in the flour and milk. Whisk the egg whites to stiff peaks and fold into the mixture. Put half the mixture into the tin at spaced spoonfuls. Fold the cocoa powder into the remaining mixture and drop in spoonfuls between the pale cake mixture. Run a knife backwards and forwards through the mixture to 'marble' it, and smooth the top level. Bake for 45 minutes. Turn on to a wire rack to cool. Sift some icing sugar thickly on the surface and cut into squares or triangles.

Caraway Lemon Cake

8 oz (225 g) self-raising flour
Pinch of salt
6 oz (150 g) butter
4 oz (100 g) caster sugar
5 tbsp lemon curd
3 eggs
1 tsp caraway seeds

Grease and line a 7 in. (17.5 cm) round cake tin. Preheat oven to 325°F/160°C/Gas Mark 3. Sieve the flour and salt together. Cream the butter and sugar with the lemon curd until light and fluffy. Add the eggs one at a time alternately with the flour. Fold in the remaining flour and caraway seeds. Spoon into the tin. Bake for 1 hour. Leave in the tin for 15 minutes, then turn out on to a wire rack to cool.

Sand Cake

This is one of the most delicious 'plain' cakes with a soft melting texture. If potato flour is not obtainable, add an extra ounce (25 g) plain flour.

2 oz (50 g) ground rice
2 oz (50 g) plain flour
4 oz (100 g) butter
4 oz (100 g) caster sugar

1 oz (25 g) potato flour
½ tsp baking powder
Pinch of salt
2 eggs
A little icing sugar

Grease and lightly flour and sugar a 1 lb (450 g) loaf tin. Preheat oven to 375°F/190°C/Gas Mark 5. Sieve the rice, flour, potato flour, baking powder and salt into a bowl. Cream the butter and sugar until light and fluffy. Separate the eggs and beat the egg yolks, one at a time, into the creamed mixture. Fold in the dry ingredients. Whisk the egg whites to soft peaks and fold into the cake mixture. Put into the tin and bake for 40 minutes. Turn on to a wire rack to cool. When cold, dust the top thickly with sieved icing sugar.

Soda Cake

Eliza Acton (1855 edition) describes Soda Cake as resembling Pound Cake if carefully made, but having the advantages of being 'much less expensive, far more wholesome, while it has the advantage of being very expeditiously prepared'. It is important not to add too much soda which can impart an unpleasant flavour. The cake is indeed an economical one using only one egg since the soda does the work of raising the cake.

8 oz (225 g) plain flour
Pinch of salt
1 tsp bicarbonate of soda
½ tsp cream of tartar
Pinch of ground nutmeg *or* a little grated lemon rind
4 oz (100 g) butter *or* margarine
4 oz (100 g) caster sugar
6 oz (150 g) currants
1 egg
¼ pt (150 ml) milk

Grease and flour a 7 in. (17.5 cm) round cake tin. Preheat oven to 375°F/190°C/Gas Mark 5. Sieve the flour, salt, soda, cream of tartar and nutmeg into a basin. Rub in the butter until the mixture is like fine breadcrumbs. Stir in the sugar and currants and mix well. Beat the egg and milk together and add to the dry ingredients to make a fairly soft mixture. Put into the tin and bake for 20 minutes. Reduce heat to 350°F/180°C/Gas Mark 4 and continue cooking for 30 minutes. Leave in tin for 5 minutes, then turn on to a wire rack to cool.

Walnut and Pineapple Cake

The lovely mixture of crunchy walnuts and soft pineapple makes this an attractive cake, which is very good as a substitute for a heavy, richly fruited Christmas cake.

8 oz (225 g) unsalted butter
8 oz (225 g) caster sugar
12 oz (350 g) plain flour
2 tsp baking powder
Pinch of ground nutmeg
5 eggs
8 oz (225 g) glacé pineapple
4 oz (100 g) walnut pieces

Grease and line a 10 in. (25 cm) round cake tin. Preheat oven to 350°F/180°C/Gas Mark 4. Prepare the walnuts by toasting them in the oven for 4 minutes, then rub off the brown skins and chop the nuts coarsely. Cream the butter and sugar until light and fluffy. Sieve together the flour, baking powder and nutmeg. Beat the eggs lightly. Add the dry ingredients and the eggs alternately to the creamed mixture. Chop the glacé pineapple into small pieces and fold in with the nuts. Put into the tin and bake for 1½ hours, covering the cake with paper after the first hour if it is becoming too brown. Leave in tin for 5 minutes, then turn out on to a wire rack to cool. The cake may be dusted with sieved icing sugar, but for a more special occasion it may be finished with Royal Icing (p. 169) or Fluffy Frosting (p. 120).

Almond Cake

Another of those deliciously flavoured plain cakes which are so good with tea, coffee, or a glass of Madeira in the Victorian style.

8 oz (225 g) plain flour
1 oz (25 g) ground rice
1 oz (25 g) ground almonds
1 tsp baking powder
Pinch of salt
8 oz (225 g) unsalted butter
8 oz (225 g) caster sugar
4 eggs
4 tbsp dry sherry
4 drops almond *or* ratafia essence

Grease and lightly flour an 8 in. (20 cm) round cake tin. Preheat oven to 350°F/180°C/Gas Mark 4. Sieve the flour, rice, almonds, baking powder and salt together. Cream the butter and sugar until light and fluffy. Beat the eggs lightly together and add alternately with the dry ingredients to the creamed mixture. Stir in the sherry and essence. Put into the tin and bake for 1 hour 15 minutes. Leave in tin for 5 minutes and then turn on to a wire rack to cool.

Marmalade Cake

This is a very quickly made cake, and an old favourite with its subtle orange flavour. This flavour may however be varied considerably with the type of marmalade used and I prefer a rich dark chunky variety. Lemon marmalade also gives a very good flavour. If the pieces of orange peel are rather large chop them finely before use.

4 oz (100 g) butter
4 oz (100 g) caster sugar
2 eggs
4 oz (100 g) self-raising flour
2 rounded tbsp marmalade

Grease and lightly flour a 6 in. (15 cm) round cake tin. Preheat oven to 350°F/180°C/Gas Mark 4. Cream the butter and sugar until light and fluffy, and then beat in the eggs one at a time. Sieve the flour and fold into the mixture. Stir in the marmalade until well-blended into the mixture. Put into the tin and bake for 1 hour. Leave in tin for 5 minutes, then turn on to a wire rack to cool.

Coconut Cake

10 oz (300 g) plain flour
1 tsp baking powder
Pinch of salt
2 oz (50 g) desiccated coconut
1 orange
5 oz (125 g) butter
6 oz (150 g) caster sugar
2 eggs

Grease and line a 7 in. (17.5 cm) round cake tin. Preheat oven to 350°F/180°C/Gas Mark 4. Sieve the flour with baking powder and salt. Stir in the coconut. Grate the rind and squeeze the juice from the orange. Stir the rind into the flour mixture. Cream the butter and sugar until light and fluffy. Beat the eggs lightly together. Add the dry ingredients and the eggs alternately to the creamed mixture. Finally, beat in the orange juice. Put into the tin and bake for 1½ hours. Turn out and cool on a wire rack.

Cherry Cake

Cherry Cake, lightly flavoured with almond and lemon, is an all-time favourite, but it can be a disappointment if all the cherries have sunk to the bottom. The secret of success is to wash the cherries in a little hot water and then to dry them thoroughly on kitchen paper before cutting in halves or quarters and tossing in a little of the flour.

6 oz (150 g) plain flour
2 oz (50 g) ground almonds
½ tsp baking powder
5 oz (125 g) unsalted butter
5 oz (125 g) caster sugar
2 eggs
3 oz (75 g) glacé cherries
2 tbsp milk
Few drops of lemon essence

Grease and lightly flour a 6 in. (15 cm) round cake tin. Preheat oven to 350°F/180°C/Gas Mark 4. Prepare the cherries by placing them in a bowl and pouring on a few drops of boiling water. Drain well and dry on kitchen paper. Cut into halves or quarters and toss in 1 oz (25 g) flour. Sieve the remaining flour, almonds and baking powder. Cream the butter and sugar until light and fluffy and beat in each egg separately. Fold in the dry ingredients and then the cherries and any remaining flour. Mix well with the milk and lemon essence. Put into the tin and bake for 1 hour.

Dorset Apple Cake

The county of Hardy's novels is rich agricultural country which has the advantages of combining the soft rolling warmth of the West Country with the more bracing south of England. Here are dairy herds and fishing fleets, watercress farms and, of course, apple orchards. This unusual cake contains chunks of apple which give it moisture, and a delicious filling, and it is just the thing for winter tea by the fire.

8 oz (225 g) self-raising flour
Pinch of salt
4 oz (100 g) margarine
12 oz (350 g) cooking apples
4 oz (100 g) sugar
2 oz (50 g) currants
2 tbsp milk
3 oz (75 g) butter
1 oz (25 g) demerara sugar

Grease two 7 in. (18 cm) sponge sandwich tins. Preheat oven to 425°F/220°C/Gas Mark 7. Sift the flour and salt together. Rub in the margarine until the mixture is like fine breadcrumbs. Peel and core the apples and chop them in 1 in. (2.5 cm) cubes. Stir into the flour with the sugar and currants. Mix in the milk to give a stiff dough. Divide the cake mixture between the tins. Bake for 10 minutes. Reduce heat to 300°F/150°C/Gas Mark 2 and continue baking for 1 hour. Turn out and cool for 10 minutes. Divide the butter in half. Cream half the butter with the demerara sugar until just mixed but the sugar has not melted into the butter. Sandwich the cakes together with the plain butter. Spread the sugar mixture on top and serve at once.

Somerset Cider Cake

Dry cider gives this plain cake a delicious flavour and the cake is moist and succulent.

4 oz (100 g) butter
4 oz (100 g) light soft brown sugar
9 oz (250 g) plain flour
1 tsp bicarbonate of soda
½ tsp ground nutmeg
2 eggs
½ pt (300 ml) dry cider

Grease and line a 7 in. (17.5 cm) round cake tin. Preheat oven to 375°F/190°C/Gas Mark 5. Cream the butter and sugar until light and fluffy. Sieve together the flour, soda and nutmeg. Beat the eggs lightly. Add the flour and the eggs alternately to the creamed mixture until incorporated, beating well with each addition. Gradually add the cider, beating all the time. Put into the tin and bake for 1¼ hours. Leave in tin for 5 minutes, then turn on to a wire rack to cool.

Somerset Apple Cake

The name 'Somerset' means 'the county of the summer farm dwellers', and in the summer the farmhouses and cottages used to be surrounded by trees full of ripening apples. Somerset is the home of scrumpy – farmhouse cider – and on Old Twelfth Night (17 January) the apple trees are wassailed or wished 'good health' by the villagers. This has been practised for centuries by farmers warding off the evil spirits from their precious crops. Cider is poured on the roots of one of the best trees, and the trees are shot at with guns. Naturally, apples play a large part in the cooking of the area.

8 oz (225 g) plain flour
1 tsp baking powder
3 oz (75 g) lard
1 lb (450 g) cooking apples
1 egg
2 oz (50 g) black treacle

Grease a 10 × 7 in. (25 × 18 cm) tin. Preheat oven to 350°F/180°C/Gas Mark 4. Sift together the flour and baking powder. Rub in the lard until the mixture is like fine breadcrumbs. Peel and core the apples and put them through the coarse blade of a mincer. Beat the egg into the flour mixture and add the minced apples and treacle. Work together to make a stiff and sticky dough. Put into the tin and bake for 35 minutes. Cut into squares while hot. Leave in the tin for 5 minutes, then lift out on to a wire rack to cool. Serve split and buttered, and dusted with caster sugar.

Wholemeal Dripping Cake

This hearty cake is probably very close to the first kind of fruit cake enjoyed by our ancestors before flour, sugar or fat were refined.

8 oz (225 g) mixed dried fruit and peel
3 oz (75 g) clarified beef dripping*
5 oz (125 g) light soft brown sugar
8 fl oz (225 ml) water
8 oz (225 g) wholemeal flour
1 tsp baking powder
½ tsp bicarbonate of soda
Pinch of ground nutmeg
Pinch of ground cinnamon
Pinch of ground mixed spice

Grease a 6 in. (15 cm) round cake tin. Preheat oven to 350°F/180°C/Gas Mark 4. Put the fruit, dripping, sugar and water into a thick saucepan. Bring to the boil, then reduce the heat and simmer for 10 minutes. Sift together the flour, baking powder, bicarbonate of soda and spices. Blend in the fruit mixture until well mixed but do not beat. Put the cake mixture into the tin and bake for 1¼ hours. Cool in the tin for 5 minutes, then turn onto a wire cake rack to finish cooling.

*Warm beef dripping until just liquid and pour it into a bowl containing ½ pint (300 ml) boiling water. Stir for 4 minutes and then leave to get cold. Impurities will sink to the bottom and the solid dripping will be pure and smooth and suitable for use in cakes or pastry.

Orange Walnut Cake

Sweet oranges had been grown in eastern Mediterranean lands since medieval times, but their flavour was not good. During the sixteenth century, the Portuguese brought back a superior sweet orange from Ceylon and this type became more widely cultivated. A hundred years later the Portuguese found even better China oranges with sweet skins which were suitable for preserving, and these became the most popular import to England. Sir Francis Carew is said to have grown the first orange trees in England in 1568 near Croydon, and Samual Pepys had some orange trees growing in a garden in Hackney in 1666. Until the twentieth century citrus fruit was mainly imported in the winter months and was a special treat, but so many countries now grow oranges that they can always be in season. This light moist cake has a delicious flavour of fresh orange.

6 oz (150 g) butter
Grated rind of 1 orange
6 oz (150 g) caster sugar
2 eggs
10 oz (300 g) self-raising flour
2 oz (50 g) orange marmalade
2 oz (50 g) chopped candied orange peel
3 oz (75 g) chopped walnuts
5 tbsp water

Grease and flour a 7 in. (18 cm) round cake tin. Preheat oven to 350°F/180°C/Gas Mark 4. Cream the butter, orange rind and sugar with a wooden spoon until light and fluffy. Beat the egg yolks into the creamed mixture one at a time with a teaspoonful of flour each time. Stir in the marmalade, peel and nuts and the water, and mix thoroughly. Fold in the flour. Whisk the egg whites to stiff peaks and fold into the cake mixture. Put the cake mixture into the tin. Bake for 1¼ hours. Cool in the tin for 5 minutes, then turn on to a wire rack to finish cooling.

Seed Cake

In medieval times the seeds of herbs such as aniseed and caraway were popular flavourings for bread, and for yeast-raised cakes. Caraway, with its slightly medicinal and refreshing flavour, remained popular for centuries. Seed cakes were great favourites in the eighteenth century, when most cakes were still made with yeast. However, eggs were being recognised as a raising agent, and caraway seeds proved less weighty than dried fruit for these lighter cakes. The richest seed cakes included candied peel and sack or brandy, but in those days the flavouring was added in the form of caraway comfits – tiny sweets made from the seeds covered with twelve separate coats of sugar syrup. Comfit-making was a skilled art which required plenty of time, and it died out when sweetmaking became a factory process at the end of the nineteenth century. Today we flavour with uncoated caraway seeds, but this version of the cake retains the eighteenth-century peel and brandy.

Cake
8 oz (225 g) self-raising flour
Pinch of ground nutmeg
1 tsp caraway seeds
8 oz (225 g) butter
8 oz (225 g) caster sugar
5 eggs
3 oz (75 g) chopped candied orange peel
2 tbsp brandy

Topping
2 tsp caster sugar
½ tsp caraway seeds
3 tsp icing sugar, sieved

Grease and base-line a 7 in. (17.5 cm) round cake tin. Preheat oven to 350°F/180°C/Gas Mark 4. Sieve the flour and the nutmeg and stir in the caraway seeds. Cream the butter and sugar with a wooden spoon until light and fluffy. Separate the eggs. Add the yolks, one at a time, to the creamed mixture alternating with a teaspoon of the flour each time. Add the peel and fold in the remaining flour. Whisk the egg whites to soft peaks and fold into the cake mixture. Stir in the brandy. Put the mixture into the cake tin. Mix the caster sugar and caraway seeds and sprinkle on the cake. Bake for 1¼ hours. Cool in the tin for 10 minutes, then turn out and finish cooling on a wire rack. Sprinkle with icing sugar.

Madeira Cake

The island of Madeira was colonised by the Portuguese in 1421, and they replaced the natural forest with Cretan grapevines and Sicilian sugar cane. From these crops grew the wine industry, and Madeira malmsey was a favourite wine in the fifteenth and sixteenth centuries. It remained popular in England and was a particular favourite of Victorian ladies to be taken as a mid-morning restorative with a sweet biscuit or plain cake. Madeira cake, which is more solid than sponge cake but contains no fruit or strong flavouring, is ideal for this purpose.

4 oz (100 g) butter
4 oz (100 g) caster sugar
8 oz (225 g) plain flour
2 oz (50 g) ground rice
1 tsp cream of tartar
1 tsp bicarbonate of soda
¼ tsp salt
Grated rind and juice of ½ lemon
4 eggs
2 slices candied peel

Grease and base-line a 7 in. (17.5 cm) round cake tin. Preheat oven to 350°F/180°C/Gas Mark 4. Cream the butter and sugar with a wooden spoon until light and fluffy. Sift together the flour, ground rice, cream of tartar, soda and salt. Work into the creamed mixture until completely mixed. Beat in the lemon rind and juice. Separate the eggs and add the yolks to the creamed mixture. Whisk the egg whites to soft peaks and fold into the cake mixture. Put into the tin and bake for 45 minutes. Open the oven door carefully, draw the cake out a little way and place the candied peel on the top. Continue baking for 25 minutes. Cool in the tin for 10 minutes, then turn out on a wire rack to finish cooling.

Welsh Shearing Cake

Summer shearings were once the scene of big gatherings of many small farmers sharing the work between them, and the narrow lanes would be filled with flocks of sheep going from home to the favoured yard where the shearers would set up shop. All the farm wives were busy preparing for this day, each contributing her speciality towards the baking which filled the table around which all the men would sit. Young daughters and their mothers would wait on the men to get them fed well and quickly so that the work could proceed without hindrance. Only when the men had left the table to go back to the yards would they sit down to enjoy food and chat in the excitement and importance of it all. The Shearing Cake was always served on this day.

8 oz (225 g) plain flour
8 oz (225 g) wholemeal flour
2 tsp baking powder
1 tsp ground nutmeg
Pinch of salt
8 oz (225 g) butter
8 oz (225 g) light soft brown sugar
2 tbsp honey
1 tbsp caraway seeds
1 lemon
½ pt (300 ml) milk
2 eggs

Grease and line a 9 in. (22.5 cm) round cake tin. Preheat oven to 350°F/180°C/Gas Mark 4. Stir together the flours, baking powder, nutmeg and salt. Rub in the butter until the mixture is like fine breadcrumbs. Stir in the sugar, honey and caraway seeds. Grate the rind and squeeze the juice from the lemon and stir into the mixture. Beat the milk and eggs together lightly and work into the mixture, beating well. Put into the cake tin and bake for 30 minutes. Reduce heat to 300°F/180°C/Gas Mark 2 and continue baking for 1½ hours. Leave in tin for 5 minutes, then turn on to a wire rack to cool.

8 *Sponge Cakes*

By that which lately hapnd Una saw
That this her knight was feeble and too faint. . . .
Therefore to cherish him with diets daint,
She cast to bring him where he chearen might,
till he recovered had his late decayed plight.

(Spenser, *Faerie Queene*)

Sponge cakes were latecomers to the British kitchen, for it was extremely difficult to bake such light cakes in temperamental ovens. The earliest form of sponge was probably one made to a recipe in a cookery book of 1596, in which four eggs were beaten together for two hours before being added to fine biscuit-bread. Gervase Markham included aniseed in a similar recipe which involved fine flour and fine sugar, both extremely difficult to achieve in the seventeenth century, and his cake could be served whole or in slices.

Towards the end of the eighteenth century, when the controllable oven was introduced, the whisked sponge cake became popular and was the ideal accompaniment to rich Georgian creams and jellies. Its lightness led to the name of 'diet bread' because the cake could be easily digested by invalids and those who disliked heavy foods. The cake was still difficult to achieve without mechanical aids, since the flour had to be dried and sifted, and the sugar had to be double-refined from the large sugar loaf. Eggs were beaten with the bare hand or birch twigs before the metal whisk was devised, and often the cook was recommended to 'beat for 3 hours'. The Victorians found that the addition of fat to the simple sponge mixture made a slightly more substantial cake which kept better and provided a vehicle for jam, cream or icings, and this was named in honour of Queen Victoria who enjoyed the new fashion for tea parties. This type of sponge cake became a 'sandwich' since two layers sandwiched the filling, and this name is still used to distinguish the fatted sponge from the whisked variety.

A more refined version of the sponge cake was the Savoy Cake or Savoy Biscuit introduced from Europe. The method of beating egg and sugar over heat was recorded at the end of the seventeenth century and the resulting sponge was known as French sweet bread. The same ingredients and method were used to make a *biscuit de Savoie* in which the egg yolks and whites were beaten separately (*biscuit* is the word used on the Continent for a type of light sugary sponge cake). This sponge mixture was used for finger-shaped biscuits which were popular to accompany light dishes, and also formed the basis of Charlottes and trifles. Large Savoy Cakes were made in elaborately shaped moulds and were used as the centrepiece of displays of puddings and fruit, or were soaked in wine and spirits to form Tipsy Cakes and other Victorian delights.

Whisked Sponge

As this sponge cake contains no fat it is best eaten freshly baked. It is particularly nice sandwiched with jam or lemon curd, or with jam and whipped cream, but is too light to pair with butter icing.

3 eggs
3 oz (75 g) caster sugar
3 oz (75 g) plain flour
½ tsp baking powder

Grease and base-line two 7 in. (17.5 cm) sponge sandwich tins. Preheat oven to 350°F/180°C/Gas Mark 4. Separate the eggs and whisk the yolks and caster sugar until very light and fluffy. Sieve the flour and baking powder together. Whisk the egg whites to stiff peaks. Fold the flour and egg whites alternately into the yolk mixture. Divide between the tins. Bake for 25 minutes. Leave in the tins for 2 minutes, then turn onto a wire rack to cool. Sandwich together with the chosen filling and dust lightly with caster sugar.

Sponge Fingers

Many delicious English puddings are made with a 'wall' of sponge fingers, but nowadays Boudoir Biscuits from a packet are often used. An old-fashioned, slightly misshapen sponge finger does, however, have a delicious sugary softness which is totally lacking from the commercial variety. The sponge fingers may also be served with fruit compotes, jellies or creams, or may be sandwiched together with jam, butter icing or whipped cream.

3 eggs
2½ oz (65 g) caster sugar
2½ oz (65 g) plain flour
Vanilla essence

Grease a baking sheet and dust with flour and caster sugar. Preheat oven to 350°F/180°C/Gas Mark 4. Separate the eggs and whisk the yolks and sugar together until very light and fluffy. Whisk the egg whites to stiff peaks. Sieve the flour. Fold the flour into the yolks with half the egg whites, and flavour lightly with vanilla essence. Fold in the remaining egg whites. Put the mixture into an icing bag fitted with a medium sized pipe. Pipe finger-lengths on to the prepared baking sheet. Bake for 7 minutes. Cool on a wire rack.

Savoy Cake

This very light sponge used to be made in decorative moulds and would form the basis of Tipsy Cake when soaked with alcohol, spiked with almonds and surrounded by egg custard. A very light hand is needed so that air is not beaten out of the sponge and an old recipe suggests that one person should shake the flour into the egg yolks and a second person shakes the bowl below so that the flour sinks in without stirring before the whites are folded in.

3 eggs
5 oz (125 g) caster sugar
1 small lemon
2 oz (50 g) plain flour
1½ oz (40 g) arrowroot

Grease a 7 in. (17.5 cm) round cake tin or metal mould and sprinkle with caster sugar and flour. Preheat oven to 350°F/180°C/Gas Mark 4. Separate the eggs and whisk the egg yolks and sugar into a bowl over hot water until light and fluffy. Add the grated rind and juice of the lemon and continue whisking for 1 minute. Sieve the flour and arrowroot together and fold into the egg yolk mixture. Whisk the egg whites to stiff peaks and fold in. Put into the prepared tin. Bake for 35 minutes. Turn on to a wire rack to cool.

Hampshire Drops

4 oz (100 g) butter *or* margarine
4 oz (100 g) caster sugar
1 egg
4 oz (100 g) self-raising flour
4 oz (100 g) cornflour
Pinch of salt
Jam *or* butter icing
Sieved icing sugar

Grease two baking sheets. Preheat oven to 375°F/190°C/Gas Mark 5. Cream the fat and sugar until very light and fluffy. Beat the egg lightly. Sieve the flour, cornflour and salt together. Add the egg and flour mixture alternately to the creamed mixture, beating well between each addition. Fold in the remaining flour mixture. Put large teaspoonfuls of the mixture on to the baking sheets, allowing a little room for spreading. Bake for 10 minutes until golden. Cool on a wire rack and sandwich together with jam or butter icing. Dust the tops lightly with sieved icing sugar.

Geranium Sponge

Scented geraniums are a feature of many cottage windowsills. These charming potplants have delicate feathery scented leaves but inconspicuous flowers – the different varieties smell of roses, lemon, peppermint, ginger, orange and so on. When the leaves are dried they are often used on bowls of pot-pourri to scent the house, but when they are fresh they can be used to scent preserves and cakes. When apple jelly is made, half-a-dozen leaves boiled with the sugar and fruit will produce a delicately scented preserve. For sponge cakes, two or three leaves are placed in the tin under the cake mixture and removed when the cake is cooling. The light flavour of scented roses permeates the simple cake deliciously. This sponge cake has a slightly crusty surface and does not have any filling, but is very good served with fruit compotes. If the geranium leaves are not available, a tablespoon of orangeflower water may be used for flavouring.

5 eggs
10 oz (300 g) caster sugar
5 oz (125 g) plain flour
1 oz (25 g) cornflour
Grated rind of ½ lemon
4 rose geranium leaves

Grease a 9 in. (22.5 cm) round cake tin with butter and sprinkle with caster sugar and flour (about ½ oz (15 g) of each will be needed). Preheat oven to 325°F/160°C/Gas Mark 3. Separate the eggs and put the yolks into a bowl with 5 oz (125 g) sugar. Place the bowl over a pan of hot water and whisk until white and creamy. Whisk the egg whites to stiff peaks and fold in the remaining sugar. Sieve the flour and cornflour together. Fold the egg white mixture and the flour mixture alternately into the egg yolks. Fold in the lemon rind. Put the rose geranium leaves on the base of the prepared cake tin and place the sponge mixture on top. Bake for 1 hour until firm and golden. Turn on to a wire rack to cool and remove the leaves.

Swiss Roll

Like so many cakes this one receives no mention in recipe books until the end of the nineteenth century when afternoon tea was most popular, but there seems to be no particular reason why this simple and delicious sponge should be 'Swiss'. The cake needs concentration on the part of the cook as it is very quickly prepared and cooked, and must then be very speedily rolled and finished.

3 eggs
4½ oz (115 g) caster sugar
3 oz (75 g) plain flour
½ tsp baking powder
1 tbsp cold water
6 tbsp jam *or* lemon curd
2 tbsp caster sugar for sprinkling

Grease and line a Swiss Roll tin. Preheat oven to 400°F/200°C/Gas Mark 6. Whisk the eggs and sugar together until very light and fluffy and almost white. Sift the flour and baking powder together. Fold into the egg mixture with the water. Spread the mixture evenly in the tin. Bake for 10 minutes. While the cake is cooking, put a large piece of greaseproof paper on a flat surface and sprinkle it with one tablespoon caster sugar. As soon as the cake is ready, turn out on to the sugared paper. With a sharp knife, quickly trim the edges of the cake to remove hard pieces (if this is not done, the cake is difficult to roll and will crack). Roll up the cake firmly with the paper inside and cover with a tea towel so that the cake remains soft. When the cake is cold, unroll carefully and remove the paper. Have the jam just warm enough to spread easily. Spread on the cake and roll up again from a short end. Just before serving put on to a serving dish and sprinkle with the remaining caster sugar.

Victoria Sponge Sandwich

This sponge cake is one of the standbys of the English cook, but was not introduced until the middle of the nineteenth century when a number of dishes were named after the queen. The invention of baking powder in 1855, and subsequently of self-raising flour, meant that light cakes could be made quickly – earlier recipes often specify that eggs should be beaten for 3 hours. Mrs Beeton's recipe for Victoria Sandwich recommends that the mixture should be baked in a Yorkshire pudding tin, then cut in half and put together with jam or marmalade before being cut in fingers to serve as 'sandwiches'. By tradition, the fat, sugar and flour used should weigh the same as two eggs.

4 oz (100 g) butter
4 oz (100 g) caster sugar
2 eggs
4 oz (100 g) self-raising flour
Jam, lemon curd *or* butter icing
Caster sugar or icing sugar

Grease and base-line two 7 in. (17.5 cm) sponge sandwich tins. Preheat oven to 350°F/180°C/Gas Mark 4. The butter must be at room temperature. Cream the butter and sugar together with a wooden spoon until very light and fluffy. Put the eggs into another bowl and whisk them together until well mixed. Add the eggs a little at a time to the creamed mixture, beating well after each addition. Put the flour into a sieve and gently sieve it by shaking it over the creamed mixture until about one-quarter of the flour has been sieved. Fold lightly into the creamed mixture with a metal tablespoon. Repeat the process until all the flour has been used and the cake mixture will drop easily from the spoon. Divide the mixture between the tins. Bake for 25 minutes. Leave in the tins for 1 minute, then turn on to a wire rack to finish cooling. When cold, sandwich together with jam, lemon curd or butter icing. Dust the top with caster sugar or sieved icing sugar, or finish with more butter icing.

Variations
Add ½ teaspoon grated orange or lemon rind to the cake mixture or 5 drops of vanilla, orange or lemon essence. For coffee cake, add 1 teaspoon coffee essence. For chocolate cake, replace 1 tablespoon flour with 1 tablespoon cocoa powder.

9 *Special Occasion Cakes*

> Dost thou think because thou art virtuous there shall be no more cakes or ale?
>
> (Shakespeare, *Merry Wives of Windsor*)

From time immemorial cakes have been served on festive occasions to accompany alcoholic drinks. It is thought that they were originally offerings to the gods and therefore became associated with pagan and later religious celebrations, which often became mixed up with secular feasting. Our lives are marked by christening, wedding and funeral celebrations, by birthdays, Easter and Christmas, and each event is marked by a cake. Katherine Mansfield wrote:

> It's the kind of cake that might have been mentioned in the Book of Genesis. . . . And God said: 'Let there be cake.' And there was cake. And God saw that it was good.

The familiar celebration cake is an iced cake, originating in the eighteenth century when a rich fruit cake was covered with a kind of meringue mixture of whisked egg white and refined sugar. This was often applied while the cake was still hot from the oven, and often the cake was returned in the heat to become crisp. This type of icing, sometimes known as 'bliss' when applied to wedding cakes, became today's Royal Icing, and it still remains the symbol of a very special cake, many of which are included in other chapters, according to their method of making.

The slightly less 'special' cake was introduced by the Victorians who adapted the rich Continental butter icings and found that they could be used to decorate their fruit or sponge cakes. They held so many tea parties for different occasions that all sorts of rich morsels were prepared to give variety – there were tennis cakes, golf cakes and croquet cakes, Battenburg cakes and later coffee and chocolate creations, which served to make teatime special, and which could also serve as light birthday or celebration cakes.

Cornflour Cake with Caramel Icing

The addition of cornflour to a cake mixture gives a melting texture. This cake is also very pale in colour and contrasts with its rich caramel icing. If preferred, the cake may simply be dusted with icing sugar.

Cake
9 oz (250 g) plain flour
5 oz (125 g) cornflour
2 tsp baking powder
Pinch of salt
4 oz (100 g) unsalted butter
8 oz (225 g) caster sugar
4 eggs
½ tsp vanilla essence

Caramel Icing
10 oz (300 g) demerara sugar
¼ pint (150 ml) water
Pinch of cream of tartar
4 egg whites

Grease and lightly flour an 8 in. (20 cm) round cake tin. Preheat oven to 375°F/190°C/Gas Mark 5. Sieve together the flour, cornflour, baking powder and salt. Cream the butter with half the sugar until light and fluffy. Separate the eggs and beat the yolks with the remaining sugar until pale and creamy. Add this egg mixture to the butter and beat thoroughly until well mixed. Fold in the dry ingredients. Whisk the egg whites to soft peaks and fold into the mixture. Put into tin and bake for 1 hour. Turn out and cool on a wire rack. When cold, cover top and sides with Caramel Icing.

Caramel Icing
Put the sugar, water and cream of tartar into a thick pan and heat gently until the sugar has dissolved. Boil to a temperature of 240°F/114°C (when a little mixture dropped into a cup of cold water will form a soft ball). Reduce heat and continue cooking to a temperature of 270°F/135°C (when a drop in cold water will separate into threads which are hard but not brittle). Meanwhile, whisk the egg whites to soft peaks. Allow the sugar mixture to cool slightly, and pour slowly on to the egg whites, beating all the time until the mixture is of a creamy consistency. An electric hand whisk is useful for this kind of operation as it leaves one hand free for pouring the sugar syrup. This is a rich and soft icing, and should not be spread too thickly.

Tennis Cake

This was a great Edwardian favourite, although the Battenburg cake appropriated the name to appease sensitivities during the First World War (see p. 123). It is a light fruit cake which was made in a rectangular tin to resemble a tennis court. It was originally covered in almond paste, then icing or butter cream with desiccated coconut smoothed on the sides and the edge just round the top. The cake was then decorated with a pair of silver tennis racquets and balls. Today it can be finished with green icing and marked out in white like a court.

8 oz (225 g) butter
8 oz (225 g) caster sugar
½ orange
Grated rind of ½ lemon
10 oz (300 g) self-raising flour
2 oz (50 g) ground almonds
4 eggs
2 tbsp milk
2 oz (50 g) glacé cherries
1 oz (25 g) blanched almonds
6 oz (150 g) sultanas
6 oz (150 g) currants
2 oz (50 g) chopped mixed candied peel
8 oz (225 g) marzipan
2 tbsp jam
Glacé icing
Silver balls

Grease and line an 8 × 12 in. (20 × 30 cm) tin. Preheat oven to 350°F/180°C/Gas Mark 4. Cream the butter and sugar until light and fluffy. Grate the rind and squeeze the juice from the orange. Add to the butter with the lemon rind. Sieve the flour and mix with the almonds. Beat the eggs and milk lightly together. Add the eggs and flour alternately to the creamed mixture beating well between each addition until incorporated. Cut the cherries in quarters and shred the almonds. Fold the fruit and nuts into the cake mixture. Put into the tin and bake for 1½ hours. Leave in tin for 5 minutes, then turn out and cool on a wire rack.

Roll out the marzipan thinly and cover the cake which has been lightly brushed with a little melted jam. Make up icing with sieved icing sugar and just enough hot water to give a thick creamy consistency. Reserve 2–3 tablespoons icing and tint the rest with green food colouring. Spread the green icing on top and sides of the cake. Leave until cold and firm. Using a writing pipe, decorate the top of the cake to look like a marked tennis court. Decorate with silver balls.

Walnut Cake with Fluffy Frosting

Mention Walnut Cake to any middle-aged person and eyes will become misty as they remember the glories of Fuller's teashops, cinnamon toast and *the* cake which consisted of walnut-flavoured layers holding walnut butter cream and completely covered with a fluffy frosting which looked like snow and had a similar texture. No school holiday treat or adult shopping day was complete without this splendid confection, and yet it never seemed to be recorded in recipe books. Aided by my friend Shirley, with whom I used to share this treat when we were schoolgirls, and who remains as addicted to the memory of this cake as I am, I have reconstructed the recipe and I hope that this version will please fellow-sweet-tooths.

Cake
8 oz (225 g) plain flour
1 oz (25 g) cornflour
3 tsp baking powder
6 oz (150 g) butter
12 oz (350 g) caster sugar
4 eggs
¼ pt (150 ml) milk
3 oz (75 g) finely chopped walnut kernels
½ tsp vanilla essence

Filling
2½ oz (65 g) unsalted butter
2½ oz (65 g) icing sugar
1 oz (25 g) finely chopped walnut kernels

Fluffy Frosting
1 lb (450 g) granulated sugar
¼ pt (150 ml) water
2 egg whites
Walnut halves for decoration

Cake
Grease and line two 8 in. (20 cm) sponge sandwich tins. Preheat oven to 350°F/180°C/Gas Mark 4. Sieve the flour, cornflour and baking powder. Cream the butter and sugar until very light and fluffy. Beat the egg yolks and milk together, and add to the creamed mixture alternately with the dry ingredients. Fold in the walnuts and essence. Whisk egg whites to stiff peaks, and fold into the mixture. Put into tin and bake for 40 minutes. Turn on to a wire rack to cool. When completely cold, put together layers with filling. Cover top and sides with Fluffy Frosting and decorate with walnut halves.

Filling
Cream the butter and sugar together until very light and fluffy, and fold in the very finely chopped walnuts.

Fluffy Frosting
Put the sugar and water into a pan and heat gently until the sugar has dissolved. Boil to a temperature of 240°F/114°C (when a little mixture

dropped into a cup of cold water will form a soft ball). Whisk the egg whites to stiff peaks and pour on to the sugar syrup gradually, whisking all the time until the mixture is thick and almost cold (an electric hand whisk aids this process). Pour quickly over the cake and put on walnuts before the icing sets. It is very important that the sugar syrup reaches the correct temperature and that the icing is beaten hard until thick. When on the cake, it will form a thin crust on the outside, but remain soft inside.

Chocolate Rum Cake

Chocolate and rum are complementary flavours which enhance each other in sweetmeats, puddings and cakes. This rich chocolate cake is for a very special occasion.

Cake
6 oz (150 g) butter
6 oz (150 g) caster sugar
6 tbsp black treacle
2 eggs
6 oz (150 g) self-raising flour
1 oz (25 g) cornflour
1 oz (25 g) cocoa powder
4 tbsp milk
1 tbsp dark rum

Icing
8 oz (225 g) butter
12 oz (350 g) icing sugar
2 tbsp black treacle
6 tbsp milk
2 tbsp rum
2 tbsp boiling water

Grease and base-line two 7 in. (17.5 cm) sponge sandwich tins. Preheat oven to 350°F/180°C/Gas Mark 4. Cream the butter, sugar and black treacle together with a wooden spoon until light and fluffy. Add the eggs one at a time, beating well after each addition. Sift the flour, cornflour and cocoa together. Mix the milk and rum together. Fold the flour mixture into the cake mixture alternately with the milk and rum. Divide the cake mixture between the tins. Bake for 30 minutes. Turn out on a wire rack to cool. When the cakes are completely cold, split each one horizontally in half.

To make the icing, cream the butter, sugar and black treacle together until light and fluffy. Beat in the milk and rum very gradually. Add the boiling water a few drops at a time, beating well. Sandwich the layers of cake with this icing and cover the top with icing.

Dark Chocolate Cake

Although chocolate cake is one of the glories of the British tea-table, it is a comparatively recent invention. Cocoa beans were first brought to England in the seventeenth century, but were only used for making drinking chocolate. The first London chocolate house opened in 1657 and chocolate remained a luxury until 1853 when Gladstone lowered the duty on it. Originally chocolate was sold to the customer in the form of 'nibs', or the centre of cocoa beans which had to be ground, but by 1824 John Cadbury was selling prepared beans, and by the middle of the nineteenth century block chocolate was available for the housewife, which was sometimes used for puddings and confectionery. Neither Mrs Beeton nor Miss Acton, however, had a chocolate cake in their cookery books, and it seems to have been a turn-of-the-century invention. This recipe gives a rich dark cake which is light in texture.

Cake
4 oz (100 g) soft margarine
6 oz (150 g) dark soft brown sugar
2 eggs
6 oz (150 g) plain flour
1 tsp baking powder
½ tsp bicarbonate of soda
¼ pt (150 ml) Guinness
2 oz (50 g) cocoa powder

Icing and Decoration
4 oz (100 g) plain chocolate
1 tbsp milk
4 oz (100 g) soft margarine
8 oz (225 g) icing sugar, sieved
12 walnut halves

Grease and base-line two 8 in. (20 cm) sponge sandwich tins. Preheat oven to 350°F/180°C/Gas Mark 4. Beat together the margarine and sugar until light and fluffy. Beat in the eggs one at a time. Sieve together the flour, baking powder and bicarbonate of soda, and fold into the creamed mixture. Mix the Guinness and cocoa powder together to give a thick paste. Stir into the cake mixture and beat just enough to mix completely. Pour the mixture evenly into the tin. Bake for 30 minutes. Turn out on a wire rack to cool.

To make the icing, put the chocolate and milk into a bowl over a saucepan of hot water. Simmer until the chocolate has melted, and remove the bowl from the hot water. Cool until the chocolate is lukewarm. Beat together the margarine and icing sugar until soft and creamy. Beat in the melted chocolate until the icing is evenly coloured. Put one cake on a serving plate and spread one-third of the icing on it. Put the second cake on top and spread with the remaining icing. Decorate with the walnut halves.

Battenburg Cake

This cake was named after the Battenburg family, who changed their name to Mountbatten. It still retains this name in professional kitchens, but between the World Wars, when German names were unpopular, it was more commonly known as Tennis Cake for its resemblance to a tennis court. Certainly the cake is a little more elaborate than most traditional English cakes, and is evocative of the leisurely days of tennis parties and tea under the cedar tree.

3 eggs
3 oz (75 g) caster sugar
3 oz (75 g) plain flour
Pink food colouring
3 oz (75 g) icing sugar
1½ oz (40 g) butter
Few drops of vanilla essence
2 tbsp apricot jam
8 oz (225 g) marzipan

Grease and base-line an 8 in. (20 cm) square cake tin. Divide the prepared tin down the centre with a double strip of greased aluminium foil to make two oblong shapes. Preheat oven to 400°F/200°C/Gas Mark 6. Whisk the eggs and caster sugar in a bowl over hot water until thick and pale. Sieve the flour and fold into the egg mixture. Divide the mixture in half and put half into the divided cake tin. Colour the remaining mixture lightly pink and put into the other half of the cake tin. Bake for 15 minutes. Turn out on to a wire rack to cool. Beat the icing sugar, butter and vanilla essence together until light and creamy. Trim the edges of the cake and cut each piece into half lengthways. Sandwich each plain strip with a pink strip, using the buttercream. Place the strips together, alternating the colours, and fixing together with the buttercream. Roll out the marzipan to form a rectangle 7 × 11 in (17.5 × 27.5 cm) and brush with apricot jam. Place one side of the cake on the short edge and roll the marzipan around the cake. Pinch the top edges between thumb and forefinger and mark a criss-cross pattern on the top with a knife. Trim the ends. Dust the surface with caster sugar.

Coffee Fudge Cake

Coffee was introduced to Europe by the Turks. The beans originally grev
in Ethiopia and the Sudan, where they were chewed as nourishment anc
as a stimulant. An infusion of the beans was known in Arabia in th
fifteenth century and coffee-drinking spread through the Middle Eas
reaching Turkey around 1530. Travellers brought the habit to England
and John Evelyn saw undergraduates drinking coffee at Balliol in 1637
The first coffee house was established in Oxford in 1650 and the habi
rapidly spread to London, where coffee houses were licensed premises
since coffee was expensive to import and made liable to excise duty. Coffe
remained an exclusive drink until the invention of coffee essence at the
end of the nineteenth century which made a sweet cheap cup of coffee
available to all. Coffee then began to be used as a flavouring agent, mainly
for jellies and creams, but even in the early twentieth century the great
cook Mrs Agnes Marshall made no mention of coffee in her cakes and
puddings. The rather sophisticated coffee cake would seem to be a recent
invention, but it is certainly very popular.

Cake
3 eggs
3 oz (75 g) caster sugar
2 tbsp coffee essence
4 oz (100 g) self-raising flour

Filling
4 oz (100 g) butter
8 oz (225 g) icing sugar, sieved
2 tbsp coffee essence

Fudge Icing
2 oz (50 g) butter
12 oz (350 g) icing sugar, sieved
2 tbsp coffee essence
2 tbsp single cream

Grease and base-line two 7 in. (17.5 cm) sponge sandwich tins. Preheat oven to 375°F/190°C/Gas Mark 5. Put ½ pint (300 ml) cider, 4 oz (100 g) essence until thick and creamy, and the whisk will leave a trail when lifted from the mixture. Fold in sifted flour. Divide the mixture between the tins, and bake for 20 minutes. Turn out on a wire rack to cool. When cold, sandwich together with the filling, and cover the top and sides with the Fudge Icing.

Make the filling by creaming the butter with a wooden spoon until light and fluffy, and then beating in the icing sugar and essence until well mixed, and the filling is soft and creamy.

Make the Fudge Icing by melting the butter over very low heat. Add half the icing sugar and the essence and beat until smooth. Remove from the heat and beat in the remaining icing sugar. Beat in the cream until the mixture is a spreading consistency.

Taunton Cider Cream Cake

Since Taunton is the centre of a great cider-making industry, there are many good local recipes which incorporate this delicious drink. One of the secrets of cooking with cider is to reduce it considerably during cooking so that the apple flavour becomes concentrated. This cake is rather special for teatime, but is also suitable for a party pudding.

¾ pt (450 ml) medium cider
5 oz (125 g) granulated sugar
4 oz (100 g) seedless raisins
3 eggs
3 oz (75 g) caster sugar
2½ oz (65 g) plain flour
1 large eating apple
½ pt (300 ml) double cream

Grease and base-line two 7 in. (17.5 cm) sponge sandwich tins. Preheat oven to 375°F/190°C/Gas Mark 5. Put ½ pint (300 ml) cider, 4 oz (100g) sugar and the raisins into a saucepan. Bring to the boil, then reduce the heat and simmer until the liquid has been reduced to half. Remove the pan from the heat and cool to lukewarm. Cover and leave to stand for 4 hours so that the raisins become very plump and absorb most of the liquid.

Put the eggs and caster sugar into a large bowl over hot, but not boiling, water. Keep the water just simmering and whisk the eggs and sugar together until thick and creamy. The bubbles in the mixture should be small and opaque and the mixture will retain the mark of the whisk. Take the bowl from the heat and continue whisking until cold. Sift the flour and gradually fold into the mixture. Divide the cake mixture between the tins. Bake for 25 minutes. Cool in the tins for 5 minutes, then turn on to a wire rack to finish cooling.

Drain the raisins, keeping the cooking syrup. Peel and core the apple and cut it into 16 neat slices. Put the remaining cider and sugar into a pan and heat until the sugar has melted. Poach the apple slices in this liquid very gently until they are just tender but unbroken. Drain and cool the apple slices. Whip the cream stiffly.

Put one cake on a serving plate and brush with one-third of the reserved syrup. Put half the cream on top and cover with the raisins. Put the second cake on top and brush with half the remaining syrup. Arrange the apple slices in the centre of the cake and brush with the remaining syrup. Put the remaining cream round the apples with a spoon. Serve very fresh.

10 *Pastry Cakes and Tarts*

When racing and fighting were all at an end,
To an ale-house each went with a sweet-heart or friend;
Some went to Shaw's, others Phillips chose,
But me and my Moll to the Hare and Hounds goes.

Chorus
With music and cakes,
For to keep up the wakes
Among wenches and fine country beaux.

(Eccles Wake Song)

Pastry cakes and tarts have always been popular as the wall of pastry made a convenient container for delicate curds or dried fruit confections. Cheese tarts were recorded in the thirteenth century in the Countess of Leicester's household, made with soft cheese mixed with egg yolks, spices and sugar. Dried fruit was sometimes added and even minced meat to make a tart similar to our mince pie. By the eighteenth century the original milk curd was often substituted by a creamy mixture of lemon juice, egg yolks, sugar and butter, and later this lemon mixture was itself imitated by lemon-flavoured sponge cake dotted with currants, and the result was a cake rather than a tart. This type of cheesecake was sold at fairs and in the streets, and the cake was given a seal of approval by Henry VIII in the form of a Maid of Honour (p. 128).

The other type of pastry cake appears to be even older, as it is said that the Eccles Cake was first introduced by twelfth-century Crusaders. There are many variations on the fruit-filled pastry case, and there are certainly similar confections in the East, so it is possible that they come from the same source. The fruit in the various oval, triangular or round puffs of pastry is said to have a religious significance along with the spices which also came from the East, commemorating the gifts of the Magi or Three Kings to the infant Christ. Many of these traditional cakes are triangular, supposedly representing the Trinity, and mince pies were originally crib-shaped. Many of the cakes were eaten traditionally at religious festivals such as Easter and Christmas and were gifts from godparents, so perhaps it is appropriate that Thackeray, who had a passion for tarts, should have felt that tarts and pastry confections were the symbol of innocence and vulnerability.

Richmond Maids of Honour

These little cakes were first made in the royal kitchens of Richmond Palace, and Henry VIII suggested that they should be called 'Maids of Honour' after the unmarried girls who attended the queen. The girl who made them gave the recipe to Mr Billet who supplied the ingredients, and he opened a shop to sell the cakes. The business stayed in his family for generations and was sold to the Newens family who still keep a Maids of Honour shop.

1 pt (600 ml) milk
2 oz (50 g) sugar
1 tsp junket rennet
3 oz (75 g) butter
1 egg
1 tbsp brandy
½ oz (15 g) ground almonds
8 oz (225 g) puff pastry

The filling for the tart must be prepared the day before it is needed. Put the milk into a saucepan with half the sugar, and heat it gently until it is just warm to the touch, but not hot. Take off the heat and stir in the rennet, then leave in the pan for 30 minutes. Transfer to a very fine sieve over a bowl and leave in a cool place overnight. Grease twelve deep tartlet tins. Preheat oven to 425°F/220°C/Gas Mark 7. Cream the butter with a wooden spoon to soften it and work in the curds from the sieve. Beat the egg with the brandy, almonds and remaining sugar, and work into the curd mixture. Line deep patty tins with the pastry and spoon the filling into them, so that they are half-filled. Bake for 20 minutes. Remove to a wire rack to cool.

Kentish Flead Cakes

Quite a large number of pigs are reared in Kent, particularly in areas where there are cherry orchards. Flead is the inside fat of a pig, and is available on request at most good butchers. Not very long ago these flead cakes were obtainable from Kentish bakers, but they seem to have gone out of fashion now. They are a little like Lardy Cakes but much lighter. The friend who gave me this recipe remembers that when she was a child it was her job, on baking days, to beat the flead dough with a large rolling pin. In many families the children would vie one with the other to see who could beat it the hardest. Of course this was very good for the dough and was, no doubt, encouraged by mothers as it saved them the job.

10 oz (300 g) flead
1 lb (450 g) plain flour
Pinch of salt
Cold water
3 oz (75 g) butter

Flour a baking sheet. Preheat oven to 450°F/230°C/Gas Mark 8. Carefully remove all the skin and membrane from the flead, and cut into small pieces. Add the prepared flead to the flour and salt and mix well together. Put in just enough cold water to make a stiff dough and put this out on to a well-floured board. Then, using a floured rolling pin, beat well, turning from time to time. Unlike pastry, the more roughly you handle this dough the better. Leave to rest for a short time, then roll out, dot with butter, fold in half and re-roll to incorporate the butter. Finally roll out to 1 in. (2.5 cm) thickness. Cut into small cakes with a scone cutter. Put on to the baking sheet and bake for 10–12 minutes. The cakes should be firm but pale in colour and very light in texture. They are best eaten warm, and are particularly delicious served with a rich fruit jam.

Curd Cheese Cakes

8 oz (225 g) shortcrust pastry
8 oz (225 g) cottage cheese
Pinch of salt
2 eggs
2 oz (50 g) butter
4 oz (100 g) granulated sugar
1 oz (25 g) currants
1 tsp baking powder
Pinch of ground nutmeg

Grease 18 patty tins. Preheat oven to 375°F/190°C/Gas Mark 5. Roll out the pastry, cut into rounds, and line the patty tins. Sieve the cottage cheese into a bowl and beat in the salt and eggs. Melt the butter and cool. Beat into the cheese with the sugar, currants, baking powder and nutmeg. Fill the pastry cases three-quarters full with the mixture. Bake for 25 minutes. Cool on a wire rack.

Cumberland Currant Cake

It is said that rum in particular is popular with inhabitants of the former county of Cumberland because rum-smuggling was rife on the rugged coastline, and villagers took home accidentally broken casks rather than waste the contents. Certainly many favourite recipes are rich with rum which goes particularly well with dried fruit and spices.

Filling
6 oz (150 g) currants
½ tsp ground allspice
Pinch of ground mace
¼ tsp ground cinnamon
Grated rind of 1 lemon
2 oz (50 g) butter
2 oz (50 g) dark soft brown sugar
2 tbsp dark rum

Pastry
8 oz (225 g) plain flour
3 oz (75 g) butter
2 oz (50 g) lard
Pinch of salt

Grease an 8 in. (20 cm) square cake tin. Preheat oven to 400°F/200°C/Gas Mark 6. Make the filling before preparing the pastry. Put all the filling ingredients into a saucepan and heat gently until the butter has melted. Stir well and leave to cool. To make the pastry, rub the butter and lard into the flour with the salt. Do not rub in the fat too finely, as the pastry should be flaky. Add just enough cold water to make the pastry ingredients hold together (about 4 tablespoons). Roll out the pastry and use half of it to line the cake tin. Spread the cold filling in the pastry case. Cover with the second piece of pastry and seal the edges by pinching together with the fingers. Prick the surface lightly with a fork. Bake for 10 minutes. Reduce heat to 350°F/180°C/Gas Mark 4 and continue baking for 30 minutes. Cool in the tin and cut into squares.

Welsh Cheesecakes

8 oz (225 g) shortcrust pastry
3 oz (75 g) raspberry jam
3 oz (75 g) butter
3 oz (75 g) caster sugar
2 eggs
3 oz (75 g) plain flour
1 tsp baking powder
3 oz (75 g) ground rice

Grease 18 patty tins. Preheat oven to 425°F/220°C/Gas Mark 7. Roll the pastry out, cut into rounds and line the patty tins. Divide the jam between the pastry cases. Cream the butter and sugar until light and fluffy. Beat the eggs together lightly. Sieve the flour and baking powder together. Add the eggs and flour alternately to the creamed mixture, beating between each addition. Fold in the ground rice. Put a little of the mixture into each pastry case on top of the jam. Bake for 15 minutes. Cool on a wire rack.

Banbury Cakes

An early Banbury Cake recipe of 1615 recorded by Gervase Markham consisted of a yeast-raised currant dough wrapped in a thin layer of plain dough. The cakes, which have been sold in Banbury for centuries, have a puff pastry casing and a rich spiced filling of currants and peel flavoured with rum. They are oval in shape, and a local industry grew up producing special willow baskets to hold the cakes, but this has now disappeared.

8 oz (225 g) puff pastry
1 oz (25 g) butter
2 tsp plain flour
1 tbsp rum
4 oz (100 g) currants
1 oz (25 g) dark soft brown sugar
1 oz (25 g) chopped mixed candied peel
1 tsp ground cinnamon
1 tsp ground nutmeg
Milk and caster sugar for glazing

Grease a baking sheet. Preheat oven to 400°F/200°C/Gas Mark 4. Roll out the pastry thinly and cut out oval shapes about 6 × 4 in. (15 × 10 cm). Put the butter into a small saucepan and melt over low heat. Take off the heat and stir in the flour and rum, to make a smooth paste. Stir in the brown sugar, currants, peel and spices. Mix thoroughly. Put 1 tablespoon fruit mixture in the middle of each piece of pastry. Fold the long sides of the pastry over the filling so that they just overlap. Turn in the two short ends so that the filling is enclosed completely. Turn the cakes over and flatten them slightly with a rolling pin, still keeping an oval shape about 4 in. (10 cm) long. Cut three short diagonal slits in the top of each one. Put on to the baking sheet. Brush with a little milk and sprinkle with caster sugar. Bake for 20 minutes. Cool on a wire rack.

Somerset Birds' Nests

These little cakes were traditionally sold as fairings at the many fairs and revels which were held in Somerset.

8 oz (225 g) shortcrust pastry
3 oz (75 g) apricot jam
1 egg white
2 oz (50 g) caster sugar
8 oz (225 g) marzipan

Grease 18 tartlet tins. Preheat oven to 400°F/200°C/Gas Mark 6. Roll out the pastry and cut out rounds to fit the tartlet tins. Press each round into place and prick the bases lightly. Put a few dried beans in the base of each pastry case. Bake for 15 minutes. Remove beans from the baked cases. Put a teaspoon of jam into each, but do not overfill or the jam will spill over and burn. Whisk the egg white to stiff peaks and fold in the sugar. Put into a piping bag with a star nozzle and pipe the meringue mixture in a circle round the edges of the tarts. Reduce oven heat to 325°F/160°C/Gas Mark 3 and bake tarts for 15 minutes to set the meringue. Lift on to a wire rack to cool. Mould the marzipan into small eggs and fill each nest with them. Serve freshly baked.

Eccles Cakes

These pastry cakes from Lancashire were certainly eaten in the seventeenth century and were particularly associated with the Eccles Wake or holiday at the beginning of September when everyone enjoyed donkey racing, bull-baiting, cock-fighting and other rural sports. The Puritans banned such festivities, along with rich cakes and mincepies, in 1650, and there was even an Act of Parliament authorising the imprisonment of anyone eating a currant pie. Eccles Cakes were supposedly revived by a servant who moved to the town and sold cakes made to her former housekeeper's recipe, and they are still sold at The Old Original Eccles Cake Shop, described by Arnold Bennett as 'The Most Romantic Shop in the World'. Unlike similar pastries, Eccles Cakes do not contain a mincemeat mixture of cake crumbs, but they do contain a lot of currants which can be seen bulging through the enclosing pastry.

8 oz (225 g) puff pastry
2 oz (50 g) butter
6 oz (150 g) currants
1 tsp ground mixed spice
1 oz (25 g) dark soft brown sugar
Milk and granulated sugar for sprinkling

Grease a baking sheet. Preheat oven to 450°F/230°C/Gas Mark 8. Roll out the pastry thinly and cut into 4 in. (10 cm) rounds. Melt the butter and stir in the currants, spice and sugar. Put a large teaspoonful of the mixture in the centre of each piece of pastry. Fold in the edges of the pastry to enclose the currant mixture, turn over and flatten gently with a rolling pin. Cut 3 slits in the top of each with a sharp knife and place on the baking sheet. Brush with milk and sprinkle with sugar. Bake for 15 minutes.

God's Kitchels

These Suffolk cakes were made during the Twelve Days of Christmas and were especially kept for visiting godchildren, as this was the time of year when they were most likely to visit their godparents. There was a saying 'Ask me a blessing and I will give you a kitchel.'

1 lb (450 g) puff pastry
8 oz (225 g) currants
3 oz (75 g) chopped mixed candied peel
1 tsp ground nutmeg
½ tsp ground cinnamon
2 oz (50 g) ground almonds
2 oz (50 g) butter
Caster sugar for sprinkling

Grease a baking sheet. Preheat oven to 425°F/220°C/Gas Mark 7. Cut the pastry in half and roll out each piece to a thin square. Mix the currants, peel, spices and almonds. Melt the butter and mix with the other filling ingredients. Spread the filling evenly on one piece of pastry to within ½ in. (1.25 cm) of the edge. Put the second piece of pastry on top. Moisten the edges of the two pieces of pastry with water and press the edges together firmly. Mark the pastry into 2 in. (4 cm) squares with the back of a knife without cutting through the surface. Bake for 25 minutes. Sprinkle with caster sugar, cut into squares and serve warm.

Norfolk Shortcake

This is a typical country treat made from scraps of pastry at the end of baking day, and a light hand in rolling and folding ensures a delectably light result.

8 oz (225 g) shortcrust pastry
2 oz (50 g) lard
2 oz (50 g) caster sugar
2 oz (50 g) sultanas and/or currants

Grease a baking sheet. Preheat oven to 375°F/190°C/Gas Mark 5. Roll out the pastry thinly and cover half with one-third pieces of lard, sugar and dried fruit. Fold the other half over, press lightly with rolling pin and roll out again. Repeat the process twice more, but on the second occasion do not roll out the pastry again. Cut in 2½ in. (6.25 cm) squares and place on baking sheet. Bake for 25 minutes. Sprinkle with a little caster sugar and cool on a wire rack.

Cumberland Courting Cake

This dish used to have pride of place on country tea-tables on Sunday afternoons. If a young man accepted a slice, it was as good as a proposal of marriage.

Cake
8 oz (225 g) shortcrust pastry
8 oz (225 g) thick sweet apple purée
2 oz (50 g) butter
2 oz (50 g) caster sugar
1 egg
4 oz (100 g) plain flour
½ tsp baking powder

Icing
2 oz (50 g) butter
2 oz (50 g) icing sugar

Grease a 7 in. (17.5 cm) round sponge sandwich tin. Preheat oven to 400°F/200°C/Gas Mark 5. Line the tin with the pastry and spread the apple purée in the base. Cream the butter and sugar until light and fluffy and work in the egg. Sieve the flour and baking powder and work into the creamed mixture. Spread over the apple. Bake for 30 minutes and leave until cold. Cream the butter and icing sugar together until light and fluffy and spread on the cake.

Berwick May Day Tarts

6 oz (150 g) shortcrust pastry
2 oz (50 g) unsalted butter
2 oz (50 g) caster sugar
1 egg
2 oz (50 g) currants
1 oz (25 g) ground almonds
1 oz (25 g) chopped mixed candied peel
Almond essence *or* rosewater
Juice of 1 lemon
2–3 oz (50–75 g) icing sugar

Grease 12 tartlet tins. Preheat oven to 400°F/200°C/Gas Mark 6. Cream the butter and sugar until light and fluffy. Work in the egg and then stir in the currants, almonds and peel. Flavour to taste with almond essence or rosewater. Line the tins with pastry, reserving the trimmings. Divide the fillings between the pastry cases. Use pastry trimmings to make a design or lattice on each tart. Bake for 7 minutes. Reduce heat to 350°F/180°C/Gas Mark 4 and continue baking for 15 minutes. Lift on to a wire rack to cool. Mix the lemon juice with enough icing sugar to make a creamy icing. While the tarts are still slightly warm, trickle the icing over them with the tip of a spoon.

Coventry Godcakes

Another traditional cake made from rich pastry and dried fruit, made in a triangular shape, which is supposed to be a reference to the Trinity.

8 oz (225 g) puff pastry
4 oz (100 g) fruit mincemeat
1 egg white
Caster sugar for sprinkling

Grease a baking sheet. Preheat oven to 425°F/220°C/Gas Mark 7. Roll out the pastry thinly and cut into 4 in. (10 cm) squares. Cut each square across to make two triangles. Place a spoonful of mincemeat on the centre of half the triangles. Press another piece of pastry on top of each one and seal the edges firmly. Cut three slits on top with a sharp knife. Beat the egg white lightly and brush each cake, then sprinkle with caster sugar. Place on the baking sheet. Bake for 15 minutes. Eat freshly baked.

Welsh Butter Tarts

8 oz (225 g) shortcrust pastry
2½ oz (65 g) butter
6 oz (150 g) light soft brown sugar
2 tbsp single cream
4 oz (100 g) seedless raisins
1 egg
Few drops of vanilla essence

Grease 18 tartlet tins. Preheat oven to 350°F/180°C/Gas Mark 4. Line the tin with the pastry. Melt the butter and stir in all the other ingredients. Divide the filling between the pastry cases. Bake for 25 minutes. Lift on to a wire rack to cool.

Clifton Puffs

1 lb (450 g) puff pastry
1 oz (25 g) ground almonds
1 tsp caster sugar
4 oz (100 g) eating apples
4 oz (100 g) currants
4 oz (100 g) almonds
2 oz (50 g) stoned raisins
2 oz (50 g) chopped mixed candied peel
¼ tsp ground nutmeg
1 tbsp brandy
Milk and caster sugar for glazing

Grease two baking sheets. Preheat oven to 425°F/220°C/Gas Mark 7. Roll out the pastry on a board sprinkled with ground almonds and caster sugar. Fold in three and then roll out again as thinly as possible. Cut into 4 in. (10 cm) squares. Peel and chop the apples finely. Mix with the currants, chopped almonds and raisins, peel, nutmeg and brandy. Place a large spoonful of the filling in the centre of each pastry square. Fold over diagonally to form triangles and press the edges firmly to seal. Brush with a little milk and sprinkle with caster sugar. Bake for 25 minutes until golden. Eat freshly baked and warm.

11 *Small Cakes*

And Enid brought sweet cakes to make them cheer,
And, in her veil enfolded, manchet bread.

(Tennyson, *Idylls of the King*)

Small cakes of the type we know today did not appear in many early manuscript books because of the basic problem of shaping them, and of not having a suitable oven for delicate baking. The earliest small cakes were types of bread with dried fruit or honey added, and these were often fried. There were curd cakes in little pastry cases, and types of biscuit-cakes, but the Anglo-Saxon word 'cake' could have referred to enriched breads. Certainly their cakes were small as a word list equates the word with the Latin *pastillus* or small cake. Small spiced cakes were Tudor accompaniments to wine, but from slightly later printed recipes, it can be seen that these were similar to a rich shortbread:

> then take clotted cream or sweet butter . . . then take sugar, cloves, mace, saffron and yolks of eggs, so much as will seem to season your flour, then put these things into the cream, temper all together, then put thereto your flour so make your cakes, the paste will be very short, therefore make them very little, lay paper under them.

By the late eighteenth century the British cook had learned to lighten mixtures with eggs rather than with yeast. The controllable oven was coming into wider use, and there was a vast range of tinware for moulding food. There was also the inspiration of French and Italian pastrycooks and confectioners, who introduced light sugared sweetmeats such as 'Puffs' (the forerunners of today's meringues) and 'Mackroons' with a firm base derived from the medieval waffle (Chapter Twelve). The Brandy Snap also derived from the waffle, well spiced and wrapped round wooden handles, and it gradually left the fairground and came to the drawing room with the addition of whipped cream.

Originally tea and sweetmeats were served in the middle of the evening, around 8 p.m., as the ending of dinner (which might start at 2 or 3 o'clock), and serving the same purpose as the medieval 'banquet', which was a final course of fruit and sweetmeats. As commerce developed, the meal pattern changed (see Chapter One) and tea became a sociable interlude in mid-afternoon. The Victorians took up the tea-party with enthusiasm in the middle of the nineteenth century, and the small cake became a test of the cook's skill when a variety of these delicate sweetmeats could easily be handed round, admired and eaten elegantly. I suspect that the Victorian and Edwardian housewives also developed these dainty cakes for charitable purposes, when it became fashionable to hold bazaars and garden parties for the needy poor. The humble bun, rock cake or wig might be suitable for feeding the poor, but when neighbours were studying your wares, it was important to display the delicacy and refinement of Fairy Cakes or Butterfly Cakes.

Rock Cakes

These little cakes are quick and easy to make and need no shaped tins so they are very popular on cake stalls. They are best eaten while fresh and rocky as they quickly become soft when stored in a tin.

12 oz (350 g) plain flour
1 tsp baking powder
Pinch of salt
6 oz (150 g) butter
6 oz (150 g) granulated sugar
3 oz (75 g) currants
1½ oz (40 g) chopped mixed candied peel
¼ tsp ground nutmeg
¼ tsp ground mixed spice
1 egg
2–3 tbsp milk

Grease and lightly flour a baking sheet. Preheat oven to 375°F/190°C/Gas Mark 5. Sieve the flour, baking powder and salt together. Rub in the butter until the mixture is like fine breadcrumbs. Stir in the sugar, currants, peel and spices. Beat the egg and stir into the dry ingredients and add just enough milk to make a stiff mixture. Place rocky heaps of mixture on the baking sheet with the aid of two forks. Bake for 15 minutes, then cool on a wire rack.

Irish Johnny Cakes

6 oz (150 g) medium oatmeal
2 oz (50 g) plain flour
1½ tsp baking powder
3 oz (75 g) butter *or* margarine
1 tbsp milk
3 oz (75 g) honey
1 egg
2 oz (50 g) currants

Grease a baking sheet. Preheat oven to 400°F/200°C/Gas Mark 6. Stir together oatmeal, flour and baking powder and rub in the fat. Warm the milk and honey together and pour into the flour. Add the beaten egg and mix well. Stir in the currants until evenly distributed. Put in small heaps on the greased baking sheet allowing at least 2 in. (5 cm) between them. Bake for 20 minutes. Cool on a wire rack, and eat freshly baked.

Brandy Snaps

These popular biscuits were once sold as 'fairings' along with other kinds of gingerbreads such as Cornish Fairings (p. 155), but were commonly known as Jumbles (p. 152). They used to be eaten plain, but today are more commonly filled with whipped cream. They are not difficult to make, but need a little practice to make them perfect.

2 oz (50 g) golden syrup
1½ oz (40 g) caster sugar
2 oz (50 g) butter
1½ oz (40 g) plain flour
1 tsp ground ginger
1 tsp brandy

Grease two baking sheets. Preheat oven to 350°F/180°C/Gas Mark 4. Put the syrup, butter and sugar into a thick saucepan and heat gently until the sugar has melted and the mixture is smooth. Sieve the flour and ginger. Take the saucepan from the heat and mix in the flour and the brandy. Put the mixture on to the baking sheet in teaspoonfuls, allowing 3 in. (7.5 cm) between them. Bake for 10 minutes. The biscuits will look very thin and lacy. Leave for 2 minutes on the tin. Remove each one carefully with a palette knife and wrap around the handle of a wooden spoon. Remove and cool on a wire rack. If the biscuits become brittle on the tray put back in the oven for a minute to soften again. If the brandy snaps are to be filled with whipped cream this should be done just before serving.

Macaroons

Almonds were introduced to Britain by the Romans, who thought that the nuts had a sobering effect when they were drinking wine. It is said that 'macaroon' comes from a Greek word *makaria* (happy) and that the Greeks first prepared these biscuits and sent them to Naples in the tenth century. They reached England in the seventeenth century and are still traditionally served with sherry or wine.

8 oz (225 g) caster sugar
4 oz (100 g) ground almonds
1 oz (25 g) ground rice
2 egg whites
Rice paper
1 oz (25 g) split almonds

Line two baking sheets with rice paper. Preheat oven to 350°F/180°C/Gas Mark 4. Stir together the sugar, almonds and ground rice. Whisk the egg whites to stiff peaks. Fold in the almond mixture. Put teaspoonfuls of the mixture on the rice paper, leaving room to spread. Place a split almond on each biscuit. Bake for 30 minutes. Trim excess rice paper from the edges of the biscuits and cool on a wire rack.

Fairy Cakes

These little tiny sponge cakes must be 'fairy' cakes because they are so delicate. Their flavour may be varied with a topping of sliced peel or almonds but most people enjoy them just as they are.

2 oz (50 g) butter or margarine
2 oz (50 g) caster sugar
1 egg
3 drops vanilla essence
2 oz (50 g) self-raising flour
1 tbsp milk

Arrange 12 paper cases in tartlet tins so that they remain in shape when filled. Preheat oven to 375°F/190°C/Gas Mark 5. Cream the butter or margarine with the sugar until light and fluffy. Add the egg and beat in until creamy. Stir in the essence and then fold in the flour. Add the milk to give a soft dropping consistency. Divide the mixture between the greased bun tins, or put into paper cases on a baking sheet. Bake for 12 minutes. Remove to a wire rack to cool, leaving the cakes in the paper cases.

Queen Cakes
Stir in 2 oz (50 g) currants with the flour.

Butterfly Cakes
Cool and slice the tops off just below where they have risen. Cut the tops in half. Put a teaspoon of butter icing down the centre of each cake, and arrange the slices like wings with rounded edges outwards. Dust with a little sieved icing sugar.

Raspberry Buns

These little buns are not as popular as they used to be, but they were known to generations of domestic science students and schoolgirls. At my school we were all considered too academic to tangle with a stove except when our final examinations were safely out of the way. At the age of eighteen I was given my one and only domestic science lesson, and made Raspberry Buns, which were presumably thought to be lady-like and not too taxing for the tired brainbox.

8 oz (225 g) plain flour
2 tsp baking powder
Pinch of salt
3 oz (75 g) butter *or* margarine
4 oz (100 g) caster sugar
6 tbsp milk
3 oz (75 g) raspberry jam
Additional caster sugar

Grease and lightly flour a baking sheet. Preheat oven to 375°F/190°C/Gas Mark 5. Sieve the flour, baking powder and salt into a basin. Rub in the fat until the mixture is like fine breadcrumbs. Stir in the sugar and mix to a stiff dough with milk. Knead until smooth and then roll out ¾ in. (46 mm) thick. Cut into 4 in. (10 cm) rounds. Place a large teaspoonful of jam in the centre of each circle. Moisten the edges of the dough lightly with water, and gather up tightly to enclose the jam. Place on the baking sheet with the smooth side uppermost. Make a small cross on each with a knife. Bake for 15 minutes. Sprinkle with additional caster sugar and continue baking for 5 minutes. Cool on a wire rack.

Cattern Cakes

I have a particular affection for St Catherine, the patron saint of my old school. On her feast day, 25 November, the staff performed a play for our delight and no lessons were undertaken. Old Girls still receive news of the school in an annual St Catherine's letter. She is the patron saint of lacemakers and also of the midinettes or seamstresses of Paris who celebrate the day with great festivities. In the West Country, a lacemaking area, the day is considered to bring in the winter, and Cattern's Eve (24 November) is marked by the serving of spicy cakes with mulled ale or cider, and with wheel-shaped pies of fruit mincemeat. The significance of the cakes and pies is their shape, since St Catherine was broken on a wheel. She also gave her name to the popular firework.

8 oz (225 g) plain flour
2 oz (50 g) ground almonds
1 tsp bicarbonate of soda
Pinch of ground mixed spice
8 oz (225 g) granulated sugar
8 oz (225 g) butter
2 oz (50 g) currants
1 egg

Grease a baking sheet. Preheat oven to 400°F/200°C/Gas Mark 6. Stir together the flour, almonds, soda, spice and sugar. Melt the butter, cool and mix to give a stiff dough. Stir in the fruit and the beaten egg and mix well. Turn the mixture on to a floured board and with the hands roll out a ¼ in. (33 mm) thick strip. Cut pieces 8 in. (20 cm) long and roll round like a Catherine wheel, moistening slightly so the dough sticks together. Put on the baking sheet and bake for 15 minutes. Lift on to a wire rack to cool.

Portugal Cakes

Many handwritten books contain recipes for Portugal water, Portugal broth and Portugal cakes, probably introduced when Charles II brought home a Portuguese bride in the seventeenth century. Portugal Cakes are in fact an early version of Queen Cakes or Fairy Cakes and were flavoured with rosewater and sack. Hannah Glasse (*The Art of Cookery Made Plain and Easy*, 1774 edition) suggested that the little currant cakes would last for six months, but she thought that a better version was made omitting the flour and using ground almonds instead. *May Byron's Cake Book*, published just before the First World War, gave another version with ground almonds, orange juice and rind which is rather like a macaroon.

7 oz (200 g) plain flour
4 oz (100 g) unsalted butter
8 oz (225 g) caster sugar
2 eggs
1 tbsp rosewater
3 oz (75 g) currants

Grease 24 tartlet tins. Preheat oven to 350°F/180°C/Gas Mark 4. Sieve the flour and rub in the butter until the mixture is like fine breadcrumbs. Stir in the sugar and the eggs lightly beaten with the rosewater. Stir in the currants. Half-fill the tins. Bake for 15 minutes. Cool on a wire rack.

May Byron's Portugal Cakes

4 oz (100 g) caster sugar
4 eggs
1 tbsp rum
2 oz (50 g) ground almonds
2 oranges
Icing sugar for sprinkling

Grease and base-line a 7 in. (17.5 cm) square cake tin. Preheat oven to 350°F/180°C/Gas Mark 4. Put the sugar into a bowl. Separate the eggs and add the yolks and rum to the sugar. Whisk until white and creamy. Fold in the almonds. Grate the rind from 1 orange and squeeze the juice from both of them and beat into the sugar mixture. Whisk the egg whites to stiff peaks and fold into the mixture. Place in the prepared tin and dust with sieved icing sugar. Bake for 25 minutes. Leave in tin for 10 minutes, then turn on to a flat surface. Peel off the paper and cut the cake into 12 squares. Dust with sieved icing sugar and serve freshly baked. If liked, the tin may be base-lined with rice paper which need not be peeled off the cake. The icing sugar can then be sprinkled on the top surface to complete the cake.

Melting Moments

A delightful name for a little cake made light by the use of cornflour. Sometimes they are delicately flavoured with coffee, or there may be a blob of jam or a glacé cherry on top. This version is about a hundred years old and comes from Yorkshire. One can imagine the blushes of a rustic lad as he was offered a 'melting moment' by a shy girl or her more forward mother.

6 oz (150 g) unsalted butter
3 oz (75 g) caster sugar
2 eggs
8 oz (225 g) cornflour
1 tsp baking powder
Few drops of vanilla essence

Grease 18 patty tins. Preheat oven to 350°F/180°C/Gas Mark 4. Cream the butter and sugar until light and fluffy. Beat the eggs. Sieve the cornflour and baking powder. Add the eggs and cornflour alternately to the creamed mixture and flavour with the vanilla essence. Divide the mixture between the tins. Bake for 20 minutes. Cool on a wire rack and eat freshly baked.

Puffs

These little cakes, which are an early form of meringue, occur in many eighteenth-century manuscripts after it was discovered that egg whites could be beaten to a froth by the bare hand, twig whisk or fork and would add lightness to cakes. They were flavoured with the popular caraway seeds or with almonds or lemon and seem to have been the first cakes to be flavoured with chocolate. The puffs were very tiny and supposed to be made the size of an old 6d (2½p) piece, so that they needed very little cooking.

4 egg whites
6 oz (150 g) caster sugar
½ oz (15 g) caraway seeds

Line a sheet with baking parchment. Preheat oven to 300°F/150°C/Gas Mark 2. Whisk the egg whites to stiff peaks. Add about 1 tablespoon sugar at a time, whisking until the mixture is stiff and glossy. Fold in the caraway seeds. Place in teaspoonsful on the baking sheet, keeping the mixture as high as possible. Bake for 40 minutes until crisp and dry.

Almond Puffs
Fold 2 oz (50 g) ground almonds into the mixture, and make the puffs a little larger.

Lemon Puffs
Add 1 tablespoon grated lemon rind and 1 tablespoon lemon juice.

Chocolate Puffs
Add 4 tablespoons cocoa.

Christmas Eve Wigs

These cakes were offered to guests on Christmas Eve, and were dipped in mulled elderberry wine or ale before eating, but they were sometimes eaten in Lent. The mixture rises and curls over to resemble a wig.

3 oz (75 g) butter
8 oz (225 g) self-raising flour
1 oz (25 g) caster sugar
1 oz (25 g) chopped mixed candied peel
2 tsp caraway seeds
1 egg
A little milk

Grease 12 tartlet tins. Preheat oven to 424°F/220°C/Gas Mark 7. Rub the butter into the flour until the mixture is like fine breadcrumbs. Stir in the sugar, peel, caraway seeds and egg. Mix to a soft dough with a little milk. Divide the mixture between the tartlet tins. Bake for 20 minutes until golden. Cool on a wire rack.

Bedfordshire Wigs

Another version of the Wig, which was eaten in Bedfordshire on St Catherine's Day. Catherine Parr, widow of Henry VIII, retired to Ampthill and encouraged the making of lace in the area, and by happy coincidence the patron saint of lacemakers was St Catherine. As with Christmas Eve Wigs, the edges of these cakes rise over the tins and form thick rims, which look like the curl of wigs.

1 lb (450 g) black treacle
4 oz (100 g) butter
½ pt (300 ml) milk
1 lb (450 g) plain flour
4 oz (100 g) sugar
1 tsp bicarbonate of soda
2 tsp ground ginger
½ oz (15 g) caraway seeds

Grease 12 round shallow tins (individual Yorkshire pudding tins are ideal). Preheat oven to 350°F/180°C/Gas Mark 4. Melt the treacle and butter together in a thick saucepan until just below boiling point. Take off the heat and stir in the milk. Stir the flour, sugar, soda, ginger and caraway seeds together in a bowl, and pour in the treacle mixture. Beat well and divide between tins. Bake for 30 minutes. Cool on a wire rack.

Goosnargh Cakes

These Lancashire cakes are really spiced shortbreads with a delicious flavour.

8 oz (225 g) plain flour
Pinch of salt
6 oz (150 g) butter
½ tsp caraway seeds
½ tsp ground coriander
1 oz (25 g) caster sugar
Additional sugar for sprinkling

Grease two baking sheets. Sieve the flour and salt together. Rub in the butter until the mixture is like fine breadcrumbs. Work together until the mixture forms a smooth dough. Roll out ¼ in. (65 mm) thick and cut into 2 in. (5 cm) rounds. Place on the baking sheets and sprinkle with the spices and sugar. Leave in a cool place overnight. Preheat oven to 300°F/150°C/Gas Mark 2. Bake for 45 minutes until firm but still pale. Lift on to a wire rack to cool, and sprinkle with a little more sugar as they cool.

12 *Biscuits and Fairings*

> Biscuits play a most important part in the life of every child epicure. The story is still told of a very special uncle and aunt from far away who were taken upstairs to the nursery to see the little darling at her tea. I must have been about three years old. Ginger-snaps were then a daily treat. It was a hot day. I cannot remember why I was so nearly naked; I cannot even remember why I was so obliterated, face and eyes and hair, neck and hands, by partially melted ginger-snap that auntie drew back and decided not to kiss me. I must have been wallowing – simply wallowing; a ginger biscuit on a hot day of summer is not a thing to wallow in.
>
> (G. B. Stern, *Autobiography*)

Biscuits have always been popular, representing a small sweet snack which is not quite so overwhelming as a piece of cake, and being particularly suitable for children and those with a small appetite. The first kind of biscuit to appear in Britain was the Roman version made from a paste of fine wheat flour and water which was boiled, then spread on a plate and left to cool. This dough was cut into shapes and fried, then served with honey and seasoning. Sometimes a richer version was prepared with milk instead of water, and this type of fried biscuit or 'cracknel' survived until medieval times, and still appears in some European countries.

The medieval baker prepared various types of bread as well as the cracknels, and a kind of rusk which was bread dried out in a low oven (the word biscuit derives from *biscoctus* or twice-cooked) and this was supplied to the armed forces as an early ship's biscuit. The biscuit had developed by Tudor times into a sweetmeat eaten with a sweet wine such as mead at the end of an important meal. These biscuits included wafers which could be prepared at home in special waffle irons, or might be purchased from a waferer in the streets. Wafers (*gaufres*) had been introduced by the Normans, and Paris was famous for them in all their variety, since they were often made with a wine batter or a cheese flavouring. In England they were lightly spiced, and there was also a savoury variety flavoured with a mixture of cheese and pink roe. The medieval biscuit-bread was by then being prepared in long cylinders which were sliced after baking, then sugared and dried in a low oven and known as French biscuits. Similar confections were known as Italian and Naples biscuits and these appeared in recipe books until the eighteenth century. Sometimes the comfitmaker, who was a type of confectioner, prepared more elegant spiced biscuits, but all types were still dried in the oven and could be kept for months in airtight boxes, with the layers separated by white paper.

As ovens, equipment and cookery techniques developed, and higher quality food could be prepared at home, the biscuit developed into a more finely flavoured sweetmeat to accompany the jellies and creams of the eighteenth-century table, and to appear with the newly popular drinks of tea, coffee and chocolate. There were batter biscuits to be baked on flat tins, rolled-and-stamped biscuits flavoured with citrus fruits, dried fruit and spices, and sponge biscuits prepared in shaped tins. The delicate waffle developed into the Brandy Snap (p. 140) and into the crisp base of small cakes, and the biscuit-bread lost its yeast and became a kind of rich shortcrust pastry or type of shortbread.

Fairings were rustic biscuits particularly associated with fairs and merrymakings. These were usually a form of gingerbread (see Chapter Five), and are thought to have developed from the French *oublies* which were sold in the Paris streets in the thirteenth century by the Guild of Oublayers. These were little flat cakes, often given away on religious occasions, and later prepared in convents. The name is said to mean an 'oblation' or offering of love and affection, and the fairing was also purchased as a love token. The spiced biscuits were sold by itinerant gingerbread men or women, often flashily dressed characters like Tiddy Diddy Doll with a distinctive song or street cry 'hot spiced gingerbread, smoking hot!' (the reference to smoke and heat is to the strength of the spice). The common fairings were simple circles or squares, but grander fairings were prepared with patterned rolling pins or wooden moulds, and were then gilded and coloured with sandalwood and patterned with cloves. This gilding is said to be of religious significance since the offerings to the Lord had to be glowing and bright and the practice was certainly known in the early twelfth century.

The religious significance dimmed, but moulded fairings were still popular in the nineteenth century, the patterns being of soldiers, birds, churches, hearts and flowers and the details of the pattern were often picked out with coloured icing or currants. For centuries, fairs were associated with Saints' Days, or with important events in the rural calendar such as the Mop and Goose Fairs used for hiring domestic and agricultural workers, and were controlled by royal charter. Many of these fairs continue to the present day and occasionally simple fairings or brandy snaps are sold alongside rather crude 'home-made' sweets as a last relic of the love token. A complete 'fairing' was supposed to consist of three types of cake – gingerbread, ginger nuts and brandy snaps.

Three-Two-One Shortbread

Professional cooks always refer to the basic shortbread recipe as 'Three-Two-One' because this is the proportion of ingredients which can be so easily remembered, regardless of the quantity which is being prepared. If using a patterned wooden mould, prepare it carefully so that the finished biscuit retains a clear design. Oil the mould with cooking oil and sprinkle with flour and caster sugar. Roll a quantity of mixture into the mould and turn out on to a flat tin before baking. Repeat the preparation of the mould for each use. Rice flour or cornflour gives a fine-textured shortbread. The biscuit should always be baked in a low oven and should remain pale golden in colour.

Basic Shortbread
6 oz (150 g) plain flour
Pinch of salt
4 oz (100 g) butter
2 oz (50 g) caster sugar

Preheat oven to 325°F/160°C/Gas Mark 3. Sieve the flour and salt. Rub in the butter lightly and stir in the sugar. Knead the mixture lightly and press into the prepared mould. Turn on to a baking sheet lined with greased paper. Bake for 1 hour until the shortbread is very pale golden brown. Cool on a rack and dust with caster sugar. If a mould is not available, shape into a round by hand, or roll lightly and cut into rounds or fingers.

Fine Shortbread
Substitute 2 oz (50 g) cornflour for the same quantity of plain flour.

Ginger Shortbread
Add ½ teaspoon ground ginger and 1 oz (25 g) finely chopped crystallised or stem ginger.

Almond Shortbread
Substitute 1 oz (25 g) ground almonds and 1 oz (25 g) cornflour for the same quantity of plain flour. Sprinkle shortbread with thin flaked almonds before baking.

Pitcaithly Bannock

This is a form of rich shortbread which also contains nuts and peel, and which is made in a flat round cake.

6 oz (150 g) plain flour
1 oz (25 g) rice flour
4 oz (100 g) butter
3 oz (75 g) caster sugar

1 oz (25 g) blanched almonds
1 oz (25 g) chopped mixed candied peel

Preheat oven to 325°F/160°C/Gas Mark 3. Sieve the flour and rice flour together and rub in the butter. Stir in the sugar. Chop the almonds finely. Stir the almonds and peel into the mixture. Roll into a round flat cake about ¾ in. (1.75 cm) thick and pinch the edge all round with finger and thumb. Put on a baking sheet lined with greased paper. Bake for 1 hour. Cool on a wire rack and sprinkle with caster sugar.

Petticoat Tails

This is a favourite shortbread as it is very thin and crisp. Some say the name derives from the fact that the little cakes look like the edges of petticoats; other say that it is a derivation of 'petits gatelles' or 'little cakes'. This seems more likely as they were favourites of Mary Queen of Scots in the sixteenth century, and many items in the French and Scots kitchen were closely linked. Shortbread is enjoyed at all times, but it is always on the table at Hogmanay or New Year.

10 oz (300 g) plain flour
2 oz (50 g) rice flour
5 oz (150 g) butter
4 tbsp milk
2 oz (50 g) caster sugar
Caster sugar for sprinkling

Grease a baking sheet. Preheat oven to 350°F/180°C/Gas Mark 4. Sift the flours together into a bowl. Make a well in the middle. Put the butter and milk into a pan and heat until the butter has just melted. Pour the liquid into the well and add the sugar. Mix with the fingers and knead very lightly to a dough. Put on to a lightly floured board and roll into a circle about ¼ in. (33 mm) thick. Put an inverted dinner plate on top and cut round the edge with a sharp knife. Remove the dinner plate. Invert a wineglass in the centre of the round of dough, and cut around this to make a small circle. Keep the centre unmarked, but mark the remaining outer circle into eight segments, making a deep incision, but not cutting right through the paste. Put a piece of greased greaseproof paper on to a baking sheet and lift the two circles of dough on to it. Bake for 20 minutes until golden. Cool on a wire rack and then reassemble the biscuits on a large flat serving plate. Dust lightly with caster sugar.

Oaten Shortbread

4 oz (100 g) butter
3 oz (75 g) caster sugar
4 oz (100 g) plain flour
1 tsp baking powder
½ tsp salt
1 egg
2 tbsp cold water
8 oz (225 g) medium oatmeal

Grease a baking sheet. Preheat oven to 400°F/200°C/Gas Mark 6. Cream the butter with the sugar until light and fluffy. Sift flour, baking powder and salt. Work into the creamed mixture. Beat the egg and water together and work into the mixture. Stir in the oatmeal until well mixed. Roll out ½ in. (1.25 cm) thick and cut into fingers. Place on baking sheet and bake for 5 minutes. Reduce heat to 350°F/180°C/Gas Mark 4 for 20 minutes until crisp and golden. Cool on a wire rack and sprinkle with a little caster sugar.

Shrewsbury Easter Cakes

These little shortbread biscuits with their delicate flavouring are sometimes known as Easter Cakes or Easter Biscuits since this was the season at which they were traditionally eaten. Sometimes they are made with currants, but caraway seeds are more authentic. The necessary rosewater may be obtained from any chemist.

8 oz (225 g) plain flour
8 oz (225 g) caster sugar
8 oz (225 g) butter
¼ oz (7 g) caraway seeds
Pinch of ground nutmeg
2 eggs
2 tbsp dry sherry
2 tbsp rosewater

Grease and flour two baking sheets. Preheat oven to 350°F/180°C/Gas Mark 4. Sift the flour into a bowl and stir in the sugar. Rub in the butter until the mixture is like fine breadcrumbs. Stir in the caraway seeds and nutmeg. Work in the eggs, sherry and rosewater to make a soft but firm dough. Roll out thinly on a lightly floured board. Cut in circles with a 2 in. (5 cm) round cutter. Put on to baking sheets. Prick lightly with a fork six times. Bake for 15 minutes. Cool on a wire rack.

Bosworth Jumbles

There is a legend that this recipe was dropped by Richard III's cook at the Battle of Bosworth Field at the end of the Wars of the Roses. Rather oddly, Mrs Beeton calls a similar biscuit 'California Jumbles'.

The name, which used to be Jumbal, is derived from a gemmel or twin finger-ring as the biscuits were made to look like interlaced rings or knots. They varied from a kind of bread to a type of shortcake like this recipe, but the name was used well into this century to describe the Brandy Snaps (p. 140) bought at fairs.

5 oz (125 g) butter
5 oz (125 g) sugar
1 egg
10 oz (300 g) plain flour
2 oz (50 g) ground almonds
1 tsp grated lemon rind
Pinch of ground ginger

Grease two baking sheets. Preheat oven to 350°F/180°C/Gas Mark 4. Cream the butter and sugar together with a wooden spoon until light and fluffy. Work in the egg and then the flour, almonds, lemon rind and ginger. The dough should be soft but firm. On a lightly floured board roll the mixture with the hands into sausage shapes about the thickness of a middle finger. Cut off pieces 5 in. (12.5 cm) long. Grease the baking sheets and put the jumbles on them, curling them into S shapes. Bake for 12 minutes. Lift carefully on to a wire rack to cool.

Chocolate Bourbon Biscuits

These delicious little biscuits must be a twentieth-century invention since chocolate was rarely used as a flavouring until the turn of the century, but they are a favourite with many people and very easily made.

3 oz (75 g) plain flour
½ oz (15 g) cocoa powder
2 oz (50 g) butter *or* margarine
2 oz (50 g) caster sugar
1 egg yolk
¼ tsp vanilla essence
2 tsp water
3 oz (75 g) plain chocolate
1 tsp caster sugar

Grease two baking sheets. Preheat oven to 350°F/180°C/Gas Mark 4. Sift together the flour and cocoa. Cream the butter or margarine, and sugar, and work in the egg yolk and essence. Add the flour mixture and water to make a stiff dough. Roll out thinly on a floured board and cut out twenty-four rectangles 3 × 1 in. (7.5 × 2.5 cm). Put on baking sheets. Prick each biscuit four times with a fork. Bake for 10 minutes. Cool on a wire rack. Melt the chocolate in a bowl over hot water. Sandwich the biscuits together in pairs. Sprinkle with sugar.

Digestive Biscuits

These semi-sweet biscuits, known to generations of children as 'suggestives' are very good with cheese, or eaten on their own with tea or coffee. Some people like to eat them with a square of plain chocolate on top, but of course the chocolate can be used as an icing.

8 oz (225 g) wholemeal flour
4 oz (100 g) plain flour
½ tsp salt
2 oz (50 g) lard
3 oz (75 g) butter
2 oz (50 g) light soft brown sugar
1 egg
4 tbsp water

Grease two baking sheets. Preheat oven to 350°F/180°C/Gas Mark 4. Sift the flours and salt together. Rub in the lard and butter until the mixture is like fine breadcrumbs. Stir in the sugar, egg and water to give a soft dough. Roll out and cut into 2 in. (5 cm) rounds with a plain cutter. Put on a baking sheet and prick with a fork six times. Bake for 25 minutes. Cool on a wire rack.

Chocolate Digestives
Melt 3 oz (75 g) plain chocolate and ½ oz (15 g) butter in a bowl over hot water. When the biscuits are cold, spread chocolate on the base of each one and leave until set.

Caraway Lemon Biscuits

Tiny caraway seeds have been added to our food for centuries and the seeds have digestive qualities much appreciated by our ancestors whose diet was often heavy and indigestible. The seeds were a popular addition to biscuits and cakes when imported spices were expensive (caraway grows easily in our climate) and when fruit was not only expensive but considered rather heavy for delicate cakes.

4 oz (100 g) butter
7 oz (200 g) caster sugar
1 egg
12 oz (350 g) plain flour
¼ tsp salt
¼ tsp bicarbonate of soda
1½ tsp caraway seeds
Grated rind of 1 lemon
2 tbsp lemon juice

Grease two baking sheets. Preheat oven to 400°F/200°C/Gas Mark 6. Cream the butter and sugar with a wooden spoon until light and fluffy. Work in the egg until the mixture is smooth. Sift the flour with the salt and bicarbonate of soda. Fold into the creamed mixture with the caraway seeds, lemon rind and juice. Mix to a firm dough and shape into a roll about 2 in. (5 cm) in diameter. Chill for 1 hour in the refrigerator. Cut into ½ in. (1.25 cm) slices with a sharp knife. Put on baking sheets. Bake for 10 minutes. Cool on a wire rack.

Cornish Fairings

Fairs played a very important part in the lives of our ancestors. They were held to commemorate Saints' Days or more ancient festivals such as May Day or Midsummer Day and they were often the occasion when servants and farmworkers were hired. There was music and entertainment as well as a collection of stalls selling country produce, spices and cakes. 'Fairings' were small spiced biscuits or cakes which were a special treat in times when poor peoples' food was very plain, and these little cakes were often taken as presents to those who had not attended a fair. Cornish Fairings are still made commercially and are distinguished by their attractively cracked surfaces.

4 oz (100 g) plain flour
Pinch of salt
¼ tsp ground ginger
¼ tsp ground mixed spice
¼ tsp ground cinnamon
1½ tsp bicarbonate of soda
2 oz (50 g) butter
2 oz (50 g) demerara sugar
2½ tbsp golden syrup
1 oz (25 g) candied lemon peel

Grease two baking sheets. Preheat oven to 350°F/180°C/Gas Mark 4. Sift the flour, salt, spices and bicarbonate of soda into a bowl. Rub in the butter until the mixture is like fine breadcrumbs. Stir in the sugar. Warm the syrup until it runs easily and pour into the mixture. Work with the hands to form a soft dough, and work in the candied lemon peel. Grease the baking sheets. Take rounded teaspoons of the mixture and roll between the hands to form balls. Put on the baking sheets, allowing room for spreading. Bake for 10 minutes. Remove from the oven and hit each baking sheet firmly on a solid surface so that the fairings crack. Continue baking for 5 minutes. Leave on the tin for 2 minutes then lift on to a wire rack to cool.

Ginger Parkins

3 oz (75 g) lard
4 oz (100 g) golden syrup
3 oz (75 g) plain flour
1 tsp ground ginger
1 tsp ground mixed spice
¼ tsp bicarbonate of soda
1 oz (25 g) caster sugar
3½ oz (90 g) medium oatmeal
1 oz (25 g) blanched almonds

Preheat oven to 325°F/160°C/Gas Mark 3. Put the lard and syrup into a pan and heat just enough to melt them. Sieve the flour with ginger, spice and soda and stir in the sugar and oatmeal. Mix together and make a well in the middle. Pour in the syrup mixture and mix thoroughly. Divide into 15 pieces and shape each piece into a ball. Put on to a greased baking sheet, leaving room for the biscuits to spread. Flatten each one slightly with the hand and press half an almond on top. Bake for 15 minutes and cool on a wire rack.

Ginger Shortbread

6 oz (150 g) plain flour
1 tsp ground ginger
4 oz (100 g) unsalted butter
2 oz (50 g) light soft brown sugar
1 oz (25 g) chopped preserved ginger

Grease a 7 in. (17.5 cm) square cake tin. Preheat oven to 325°F/160°C/Gas Mark 3. Sieve the flour, stir in the sugar and ginger into a bowl. Rub in the butter until evenly coloured. Stir in the chopped ginger. Work with the hands until the mixture forms a soft dough. Press into the cake tin, using a fork. Bake for 35 minutes. Leave in tin until cold. Cut into squares or fingers and lift out of the tin carefully.

Ginger Nuts

These crisp hard biscuits have been fashionable for centuries since they were served as 'fairings' or tempting little snacks at fairs and festivals. They are rather sustaining biscuits and are sometimes known as Hunters' Nuts or Hunting Nuts—Mrs Beeton said they were so called when made in long shapes which were convenient to fit into the hunting-coat pocket. This version comes from Sunderland.

6 oz (150 g) plain flour
Pinch of salt
2 tsp ground ginger
Pinch of ground allspice
Pinch of ground coriander
2 oz (50 g) butter
4 oz (100 g) dark soft brown sugar
2 tbsp black treacle

Grease two baking sheets. Preheat oven to 325°F/160°C/Gas Mark 3. Sift the flour, salt and spices together. Cream the butter and sugar together with a wooden spoon until well blended. Work in the black treacle and then the flour mixture until the mixture forms a stiff dough. Roll out on a lightly floured board and cut into 2 in. (5 cm) rounds with a biscuit cutter. Place on baking sheet. Bake for 15 minutes. Cool on a wire rack.

Savill Ginger Biscuits

4 oz (100 g) plain flour
4 oz (100 g) dark soft brown sugar
1 tbsp golden syrup
2 oz (50 g) butter *or* block margarine
1 tsp ground ginger
1 tsp bicarbonate of soda
Pinch of salt
1 egg
1 oz (25 g) blanched almonds

Grease two baking sheets. Preheat oven to 325°F/160°C/Gas Mark 3. Stir together the flour and sugar. Melt the syrup and fat together. Add the ginger, soda and salt to the melted mixture and stir into the flour. Add the beaten egg and beat well. Form into balls about 1 in. (2.5 cm) diameter, and place on the baking sheets leaving plenty of space between them. Flatten the balls with the base of a tumbler and put a piece of almond on each biscuit. Bake for 15 minutes. Leave on tins for 1 minute, then lift carefully with a palette knife on to a wire rack to cool.

Norfolk Gingers

1 lb (450 g) plain flour
4 oz (100 g) caster sugar
4 tsp ground ginger
6 oz (150 g) butter *or* margarine
4 tbsp black treacle
1 egg
2 oz (50 g) crystallised ginger

Preheat oven to 350°F/180°C/Gas Mark 4. Stir together the flour, sugar and ginger. Melt the fat and treacle together and add to the dry ingredients. Mix well, add the egg and mix into a stiff dough. Put dough on a floured board and shape into a long roll about 2 in. (5 cm) diameter. Cut into slices ¼ in. (33 mm) thick and place on a greased baking sheet. Place a slice of crystallized ginger on each one. Bake for 15 minutes and cool on a wire rack.

Abernethy Biscuits

8 oz (225 g) plain flour
3 oz (75 g) butter *or* margarine
3 oz (75 g) caster sugar
½ tsp baking powder
1 tsp caraway seeds
1 egg
1 tbsp milk

Preheat oven to 350°F/180°C/Gas Mark 4. Sift the flour into a bowl and rub in the fat until the mixture is like fine breadcrumbs. Stir in the sugar, baking powder and caraway seeds. Beat the egg and milk together and work into the mixture to make a firm dough. Roll out thinly and cut into 3 in. (7.5 cm) rounds. Place on a greased baking sheet. Bake for 10 minutes and then cool on a wire rack.

Bachelor's Buttons

Bachelor's buttons had small shanks which fitted into holes in the cloth and eliminated any need for sewing. 'Old Maids' and bachelors have played a part in British folklore, with many traditional games naming the odd person as one or the other. A bachelor's button is still one of the silver charms contained in a Christmas pudding. Doubtless these small round biscuits were considered amusing at old-fashioned tea-parties.

4 oz (100 g) butter
6 oz (150 g) caster sugar
8 oz (225 g) plain flour
1 egg
1–2 tbsp milk
Flavouring

Preheat oven to 350°F/180°C/Gas Mark 4. Cream the butter and sugar. Sieve the flour. Beat the egg and milk together. Add flour and egg mixture alternately to the creamed mixture to form a stiff dough, adding a little more milk if necessary. Flavour to taste with a little vanilla, almond or lemon essence. Take pieces of dough about the size of a small walnut and roll in the hands to form balls. Place on a greased baking sheet and flatten slightly with the hands. Bake for 10 minutes and then cool on a wire rack.

Raspberry Jumbles

12 oz (350 g) self-raising flour
Pinch of salt
3 oz (75 g) caster sugar
3 oz (75 g) unsalted butter
1 egg
2 tbsp milk
3 oz (75 g) raspberry jam
Extra caster sugar

Preheat oven to 375°F/190°C/Gas Mark 5. Sieve the flour and salt into a bowl and stir in the sugar. Rub in the butter until the mixture is like fine breadcrumbs. Beat the egg and milk together and work into the flour mixture to form a firm dough. Roll out ¼ in. (33 mm) thick on a lightly floured board. Cut into 2 in. (5 cm) rounds. Put a teaspoonful of jam in the centre of half the rounds. Make two small slits in the remaining rounds and wet the edges. Cover the jam with these rounds and press the edges lightly. Lift carefully on to a greased baking sheet. Bake for 20 minutes and sprinkle with extra sugar while still hot.

Date Slices

5 oz (125 g) self-raising flour
5 oz (125 g) porridge oats
5 oz (125 g) butter
2½ oz (65 g) light soft brown sugar
8 oz (225 g) block dates
2 tbsp honey
1 tbsp water

Grease an 8 in. (20 cm) square tin. Preheat oven to 350°F/180°C/Gas Mark 4. Stir together the flour and the oats. Rub in the butter until the mixture is like coarse crumbs and stir in the sugar. Press half the mixture into the tin. Chop the dates finely and put into a pan with the honey and water. Simmer together for 10 minutes to make a thick soft paste. Spread on the mixture in the tin and cover with remaining oat mixture. Press lightly with a fork. Bake for 30 minutes. Cool in the tin and cut in slices.

Granthams

8 oz (225 g) plain flour
½ tsp bicarbonate of soda
8 oz (225 g) butter *or* margarine
8 oz (225 g) caster sugar
8 oz (225 g) desiccated coconut
2 tsp ground ginger
1 egg

Grease 2 or 3 baking sheets. Preheat oven to 325°F/160°C/Gas Mark 3. Sieve the flour and soda together. Cream the fat and sugar until light and fluffy. Work in the flour, coconut and ginger and then mix to a dough with the egg. Roll the mixture into balls the size of walnuts. Place on the baking sheets and flatten slightly with a fork dipped in cold water. Bake for 35 minutes. Lift on to a wire rack to cool.

Orange Jumbles

Lady Jekyll, writing in *The Times* in the 1920s, suggested that these little biscuits might easily be made by the kitchenmaid in the absence of Cook. They are faintly pink 'as the underneath of a young mushroom' and Lady Jekyll recommended that they should be the size of a teacup rim, with a curled crisp edge. They are very good to serve with ices, mousses or fruit compotes.

4 oz (100 g) caster sugar
3 oz (75 g) unsalted butter
4 oz (100 g) finely shredded almonds
2 oz (50 g) plain flour
2 oranges
2 drops cochineal

Preheat oven to 350°F/180°C/Gas mark 4. Cream the sugar and butter until light and fluffy. Add the almonds and flour. Grate the rind and squeeze the juice from the oranges. Add to the mixture and then colour with cochineal to give a very light pink tint. Put teaspoons of the mixture on to a greased baking sheet, leaving room to spread. Bake for 7 minutes. Lift off carefully and cool on a wire rack.

Golf Biscuits

These semi-sweet biscuits were very popular in the 'twenties and 'thirties, and were considered 'wholesome and nourishing, and excellent for taking out on a walking or golfing expedition'. They are in fact very good with cheese or with a small piece of plain chocolate.

8 oz (225 g) fine oatmeal
8 oz (225 g) wholemeal flour
6 oz (150 g) dripping *or* butter
4 oz (100 g) light soft brown sugar
Pinch of salt
½ tsp ground cinnamon
1 tsp cream of tartar
¼ tsp bicarbonate of soda
2 eggs

Grease 2 or 3 baking sheets. Preheat oven to 350°F/180°C/Gas Mark 4. Stir the oatmeal and flour together in a bowl and rub in the fat until the mixture is like fine breadcrumbs. Stir in the sugar, salt, cinnamon, cream of tartar and bicarbonate of soda. Add beaten eggs and mix to a smooth dough, adding a little milk if necessary so that the paste holds together. Roll out ¼ in. (33 mm) thick and cut into 2 in. (5 cm) rounds. Place on the baking sheets and prick with a fork two or three times. Bake for 15 minutes. Lift on to a wire rack to cool.

Norfolk White Fair Buttons

Both white and brown fair 'buttons' were traditionally sold at the numerous fairs in Norfolk, and are still obtainable at some Norwich bakers.

8 oz (225 g) self-raising flour
½ tsp baking powder
6 oz (150 g) caster sugar
2 oz (50 g) lard
½ tsp lemon essence
Milk and water

Grease two baking sheets. Preheat oven to 350°F/180°C/Gas Mark 4. Sift the flour and baking powder together and stir in caster sugar. Rub in lard until the mixture is like fine breadcrumbs. Add the lemon essence, and enough mixed milk and water to make a firm dough. Roll out and cut in 2 in. (5 cm) rounds. Bake for 10 minutes. Remove from oven and bang the tins hard on a table. Return to oven and continue baking for 5 minutes. Cool on a wire rack. Banging the biscuits on a hard surface during cooking gives an attractively 'cracked' surface.

Flapjacks

6 oz (150 g) butter *or* margarine
1 tbsp golden syrup
4 oz (100 g) demerara sugar
8 oz (225 g) porridge oats

Grease an 11 × 7 in. (27.5 × 17.5 cm) tin. Preheat oven to 350°F/180°C/Gas Mark 4. Put the fat, syrup and sugar into a pan and heat gently until the fat has melted. Stir in the oats. Press the mixture evenly into the tin. Bake for 20 minutes until golden. Mark into squares or fingers while warm. Cut and remove from the tin when cold.

Shrewsbury Easter Cakes

Another version of the short sweet spiced biscuits which were popular at Eastertide. These are mentioned in the *Ingoldsby Legends*.

8 oz (225 g) plain flour
Pinch of salt
¼ tsp ground allspice
4 oz (100 g) unsalted butter
4 oz (100 g) light soft brown sugar
¼ oz (7 g) caraway seeds
1 egg
½ tsp vanilla essence
1½ tbsp sweet sherry

Line two baking sheets with baking parchment. Preheat oven to 350°F/180°C/Gas Mark 4. Sieve the flour, salt and allspice. Rub in the butter until the mixture is like fine breadcrumbs. Mix in the sugar and caraway seeds. Beat the egg with vanilla essence and sherry and stir into the dry ingredients to make a soft dough. Chill for 20 minutes. Roll the mixture with the hands into small balls about the size of a walnut and place on baking sheets, leaving room for spreading. Flatten each ball of dough with the base of a drinking glass, and prick lightly with a fork. Bake for 20 minutes until lightly browned. Cool on a wire rack.

Sedgemoor Easter Cakes

It is said that the Duke of Monmouth, when fleeing after the Battle of Sedgemoor, stumbled into a ditch and was aided by a farmer's wife who felt sorry for the bedraggled peasant. She made him these biscuits to sustain him in his flight, and they became associated with the area.

8 oz (225 g) plain flour
Pinch of salt
4 oz (100 g) unsalted butter
4 oz (100 g) light soft brown sugar
2 oz (50 g) currants
½ tsp ground cinnamon
½ tsp ground mixed spice
1 egg
2 tbsp brandy

Line two baking sheets with baking parchment. Preheat oven to 350°F/180°C/Gas Mark 4. Sieve the flour and salt and rub into the butter until the mixture is like fine breadcrumbs. Stir in the sugar, currants and spices. Beat the egg and brandy together and work into the dry ingredients to make a firm dough. Chill for 20 minutes and then roll out ¼ in. (65 mm) thick. Cut into 2–3 in. (5–7·5 cm) rounds. Place on baking sheets and bake for 18 mintues until lightly browned. Cool on a wire rack.

Rout Biscuits

These tiny biscuits, like little morsels of marzipan, may be decorated with nuts, glacé cherries or angelica. They were fashionable sweetmeats to nibble with a glass of wine at 'routs' or fashionable social gatherings.

6 oz (150 g) caster sugar
6 oz (150 g) ground almonds
2 egg whites
Few drops of almond *or* ratafia essence

Grease two baking sheets. Preheat oven to 350°F/180°C/Gas Mark 4. Stir the sugar and almonds together until evenly coloured. Gradually add egg white until the mixture is smooth and firm. Put into a piping bag fitted with a star or scroll nozzle and pipe small shapes on to baking sheets. Decorate with small pieces of nut, cherry or angelica. Bake for 7 minutes. Cool on a wire rack. For an attractive shiny appearance, brush each biscuit with a little beaten egg yolk or egg white before baking.

Ratafias

These tiny biscuits are similar to macaroons in their almond flavour. An almond liqueur was also known as ratafia and was extremely popular in the eighteenth century. Ratafia biscuits were eaten with wine, but also often used as a decoration for sweet puddings such as trifles.

4 oz (100 g) caster sugar
2 oz (50 g) ground almonds
Grated rind of 2 lemons
2 egg yolks

Line two baking sheets with baking parchment. Preheat oven to 325°F/160°C/Gas Mark 3. Stir together the sugar, almonds, and lemon rind and work in the egg yolks. Put small teaspoons of the mixture on to the baking sheets and flatten them with a palette knife. Bake for 20 minutes. Lift on to a wire rack to cool.

Norfolk Brown Fair Buttons

8 oz (225 g) plain flour
4 oz (100 g) dark soft brown sugar
¼ oz (7 g) ground ginger
Pinch of bicarbonate of soda
2 oz (50 g) lard
4 oz (100 g) golden syrup
Few drops lemon essence

Grease two baking sheets. Preheat oven to 350°F/180°C/Gas Mark 4. Stir together the flour, sugar, ginger and soda. Rub in the lard until the mixture is like fine breadcrumbs. Pour in the syrup and essence and mix very thoroughly. Roll out thinly and cut in 2 in. (5 cm) rounds. Bake for 12 minutes. Cool on a wire rack.

Little Hollow Biscuits

This recipe appears frequently in old manuscript books, but always in rather large quantities, using six eggs and producing about 125 biscuits. They were probably a useful standby to serve with jellies, creams and ices, as the recipe usually specifies that they must be kept in layers in a box with paper between the layers.

2 eggs
1 tsp rosewater
6 oz (150 g) caster sugar
4 oz (100 g) plain flour
Additional caster sugar for sprinkling

Line two baking sheets with oiled greaseproof paper. Preheat oven to 325°F/160°C/Gas Mark 3. Whip the eggs and rosewater together and then gradually whisk in the sugar until the mixture is thick and creamy. Sieve the flour and fold in lightly. Place teaspoonsful of the mixture on the baking sheets, leaving space to spread. Sprinkle with caster sugar. Bake for 20 minutes. Cool on a wire rack.

Sand Cakes

This recipe came from an old Essex manuscript book and yields nice little shortbread biscuits which are very good to serve with jellies, fruit compotes or ices.

8 oz (225 g) plain flour
½ tsp baking powder
4 oz (100 g) butter
4 oz (100 g) caster sugar
Grated rind of 2 lemons
2 eggs
1 oz (25 g) blanched almonds
Caster sugar for sprinkling

Grease two baking sheets. Preheat oven to 325°F/160°C/Gas Mark 3. Sieve the flour and baking powder and rub in the butter until the mixture is like fine breadcrumbs. Stir in the sugar and lemon rind. Mix in 1 egg and 1 egg white, to make a firm dough. Roll out and cut into fancy shapes. Place on baking sheets. Brush with the remaining egg yolk. Chop the almonds finely and mix with a little sugar. Sprinkle on the biscuits. Bake for 20 minutes. Lift on to a wire rack to cool.

Waffles

Waffles or Gauffres were among our earliest cakes, probably introduced by the Normans. The cake batter was sometimes plain, or flavoured with orange flowers or lemon rind and was poured into a metal mould on a long handle. The mould was often decorated with a flower design, a motto or religious phrase. The top of the mould was closed and the waffle-irons, or gauffre-tongs, held over a 'clear, hot fire' for about three minutes on each side. The crisp wafer was then dusted with sugar flavoured with cinnamon or vanilla, and served freshly baked. Religious orders were particularly adept at cooking these wafers, which were often sold to raise funds, and nuns continue the tradition by making Communion wafers.

Waffle irons are still made and can be used over a gas or electric ring or the plate of a solid-fuel cooker, but they may also be free-standing electrical gadgets. To prepare a new iron brush the grids well with oil and then heat on both sides until the iron is so hot that if water is sprinkled on the surface it will sizzle. Whenever the waffle iron is used the surface should be brushed with oil or clarified fat before heating. When a faint haze begins to rise from the fat the batter may be poured in. Pour in enough batter to cover the under-surface of the iron, but do not overfill as the mixture rises. Close the iron and cook for 2 minutes on each side.

4 oz (100 g) plain flour
1 tsp baking powder
Pinch of salt
½ oz (15 g) caster sugar
1 egg
1 oz (25 g) butter
¼ pt (150 ml) milk

Sieve the flour, baking powder and salt together and stir in the sugar. Separate the egg and beat in the yolk and melted butter. Work in the milk slowly. Whisk the egg white to stiff peaks and fold into the mixture. Cook the waffles and place on a wire rack in a single layer. Do not pile up or they become soggy.

13 *Icings and Pastry*

The three types of icing most commonly used on traditional British cakes are glacé icing (sometimes called water icing); butter cream and royal icing used over a base of almond paste. Glacé icing is most often used to give a quick and inexpensive finish to small cakes, biscuits and sponge sandwiches. Butter cream makes a richer icing for sponge sandwiches; and may be used for putting together two halves of a cake or pairs of biscuits. Butter icing may also be used for piping designs, and for finishing the sides of cakes which are to be sprinkled with chopped nuts or grated chocolate. Royal icing sets very firmly and may be used for covering a cake and for piping, and is most commonly used on rich fruit cakes for weddings and other celebrations.

Glacé Icing

8 oz (225 g) icing sugar
Water or other liquid

Sieve the icing sugar and moisten with just enough liquid to give the necessary consistency. One tablespoon liquid will give a firm icing, 1½–2 tablespoons will give a soft flowing consistency.

For a shiny icing, put the icing sugar and liquid into a small pan and stir over very low heat until well blended.

Fruit juice (e.g. orange or lemon) may be used instead of water, or the icing may be flavoured with a few drops of essence. A little cocoa powder may also be used for flavouring. If necessary, a few drops of food colouring may be added to the mixture. The icing should be well beaten and quickly poured over the cake or it will become stiff and start to crack.

This amount of icing sugar will be needed for the top of an 8 in. (20 cm) cake. Use 6 oz (175 g) sugar for a 7 in. (17.5 cm) cake, and 12 oz (350 g) sugar for a 10 in. (25 cm) cake. To cover the top and sides of the cake, double the recipe quantities.

Butter Cream

4 oz (100 g) unsalted butter *or* soft margarine
8 oz (225 g) icing sugar

Butter has the best flavour, but soft margarine is easy to use and is suitable when a strong flavouring such as chocolate or coffee is used. If using butter, it should be soft, but not hot or oily. Sieve in the icing sugar and beat with a wooden spoon or a whisk until light and fluffy. Add flavouring and colouring to taste.

The icing may be quickly applied with a palette knife, and may be swirled with long sweeping movements of the knife or the back of a spoon. The icing looks fresh and attractive if it is not overworked or pressed down with a fork. For piping, add a little extra icing sugar to give a firmer consistency.

This amount of fat will be needed for the topping of an 8 in. (20 cm) cake. Use 3 oz (75 g) fat for a 7 in. (17.5 cm) cake, and 6 oz (175 g) fat for a 10 in. (25 cm) cake, varying the other ingredients in proportion. Allow double icing for top and filling of one layer; but treble icing for top, filling and sides.

Almond Paste (Marzipan)

4 oz (100 g) icing sugar
4 oz (100 g) caster sugar
8 oz (225 g) ground almonds
1 tsp lemon juice
Few drops of almond essence
Beaten egg to mix

Stir the sugars together and add the almonds, lemon juice and essence and stir until the mixture is evenly coloured. Add enough egg to bind the mixture and give a firm paste (1 egg should be enough for this quantity of sugar and almonds). Knead lightly on a board sprinkled with icing sugar before rolling out to fit the cake.

Egg yolks may be used for the almond paste, and the whites can then be used for Royal Icing to cover the cake. Almond paste should not be overhandled as the almond oil will come through and discolour the icing which is placed on top. The cake to be covered should be brushed with a little warm jam before the almond paste is placed on top. The paste should then be left for 48 hours to dry out before the Royal Icing is placed on it. If speed is essential, brush the almond paste with egg white and leave to dry for 15 minutes before putting on Royal Icing, and the almond paste will remain soft but not spoil the top icing.

The above recipe will coat the top of an 8 in. (20 cm) round or 7 in. (17.5 cm) square cake generously. Double the quantities to coat the sides as well. For a 9 in. (22.5 cm) round or 8 in. (20 cm) square cake, use 6 oz (175 g) ground almonds and the other ingredients in proportion. For the top of a 10 in. (25 cm) round or 9 in. (22.5 cm) square cake, use 8 oz (225 g) almonds and the other ingredients in proportion.

Royal Icing

2 egg whites
1 lb (450 g) icing sugar
1 tbsp lemon juice

Whisk the egg whites lightly, but do not over-beat them. Sieve the icing sugar and add very gradually to the egg whites. Add the lemon juice and continue beating until the icing stands up in peaks and is very white. For coating a cake, the icing should be like softly whipped cream. For piping, the icing must stand in stiff upright peaks which are achieved by beating, but not by adding more sugar. It is better to prepare this icing by hand, as an electric mixer can cause the formation of air bubbles which cannot be removed. For an icing which remains slightly soft, add 1 teaspoon glycerine.

Royal icing must be placed over a base of almond paste or it will quickly discolour. Put all the icing on top of the cake and gradually work it down over the cake, working from the centre with a palette knife. Spread the icing over the sides of the cake evenly, and then neaten the top of the cake with long sweeping movements of a straight-edged knife or ruler. Neaten the sides with vertical movements of the knife or ruler.

For a special occasion, such as a wedding, a cake should have two thinner coats of Royal Icing, not one thick layer. The first coat must be thoroughly dried before the second one is applied.

This recipe will give one coat for the top and sides of a 7 in. (17.5 cm) cake, with a little left for piping; double quantitites will be needed for two coats of icing. Spare icing may be kept in a bowl covered with a damp cloth for 2–3 days if needed for a second coat or for piping.

Shortcrust Pastry

8 oz (225 g) plain flour
½ tsp salt
2 oz (50 g) hard margarine
2 oz (50 g) lard
2–3 tbsp cold water

Sieve together the flour and salt. Cut the margarine and lard into small pieces and rub into the flour until the mixture is like fine breadcrumbs. Add the water and mix quickly to a stiff dough. Turn out on a lightly floured board and knead until smooth. Roll out to required shape and thickness according to recipe.

Puff Pastry

1 lb (450 g) plain flour
1 tsp salt
1 lb (450 g) hard margarine or butter
2 tsp lemon juice
Scant ½ pt (300 ml) iced water

Sieve together the flour and salt. Divide the fat into four pieces. Rub one-quarter of the fat into the flour until the mixture is like fine breadcrumbs, then mix to a pliable dough with lemon juice and water. Turn out on a lightly floured board and knead well until smooth. Leave to rest for 15 minutes in a cool place.

Using 2 knives, shape the remaining fat into a slab 5 in. (12.5 cm) square on a floured board. Roll the dough into a rectangle 11 × 6 in. (27.5 × 15 cm). Place the piece of fat at the top end of the dough, leaving a margin of about ½ in. (1.25 cm) along the sides and top. Fold the rest of the dough over, placing upper edges of dough together, and brush off surplus flour.

First rolling Turn pastry round so that folded edge is on the left-hand side. Press three open edges together with rolling pin to seal. Press dough across about 5 times with the rolling pin to flatten. Roll out into a rectangle 12 × 6 in. (30 × 15 cm), keeping the edges straight.

Second rolling Fold pastry in three by folding bottom third upwards and top third downwards and over to cover it. Turn so that folded edge is again on the left. Seal edges and roll out as before. Fold, turn and seal edges as before. Place pastry on a floured plate in a polythene bag and leave to rest in a cold place for 20 minutes.

Third to sixth rollings Roll out 4 more times, always turning and sealing dough as before, and resting 20 minutes between each rolling. If any patches of fat still show, give dough another rolling. Rest dough before rolling out to required thickness.

British/American Conversion Tables

American measures

3 tsp	1 tbsp
2 tbsp	1 fl oz
1 American cup (16 tbsp)	8 fl oz
1 American pt	16 fl oz

Equivalents

BRITISH	AMERICAN
1 tsp	1 heaped tsp
1 tbsp	1½ tbsp
¼ pt	⅝ cup
½ pt	1¼ cups
¾ pt	1⅞ cups
1 pt	2½ cups

Equivalent weights and measures

BRITISH	AMERICAN

Almonds

2½ oz ground	½ cup
4 oz whole, blanched	¾ cup

Apples

1 lb eating	4 medium-sized
1 lb cooking	3 medium-sized
1 lb sliced	2⅔ cups

Breadcrumbs

2 oz fresh	1 cup
2 oz dried	¾ cup

Cereals

2 oz cracker crumbs	1 cup
3 oz oatmeal	1 cup
4 oz pearl barley/tapioca	½ cup
6 oz cornmeal, cracked wheat or semolina/ground rice	1 cup

Cottage cheese

2 oz	⅓ cup
6 oz	1 cup

Cornflour/cornstarch

1 oz	3 tbsp
4 oz	¾ cup

Cream

2 fl oz	4 tbsp or ¼ cup
¼ pt (5 fl oz)	⅝ cup
½ pt	1¼ cups

Dried fruit

2 oz candied peel	½ cup
4 oz glacé cherries	under ½ cup

Currants, raisins, sultanas

1 oz	2 tbsp
6 oz	1 cup

Prunes or apricots

2 oz	⅜ cup
6 oz	1 heaped cup

Flour, plain/all purposes (sifted first)

1 oz	4 tbsp
2 oz	over ½ cup
3 oz	over ¾ cup
3½ oz	1 cup
4 oz	1 cup+2 tbsp
8 oz	2¼ cups
1 lb	4½ cups

Gelatine

½ oz	2 tbsp

Honey, jam, syrup, preserves

4 oz	⅜ cup
6 oz	½ cup

Nuts, large (i.e. walnuts)

2 oz shelled or ground	over ½ cup

Rice (uncooked)

4 oz	½ cup

Soft fruits

In the USA these are sold in pints or quarts (4 cups=1 quart)

Redcurrants, blackcurrants, blueberries/bilberries

4 oz	1 cup

Raspberries

5 oz	1 cup

Strawberries

6 oz	1 cup

Cherries

1 lb	2 cups

Solid fats

1 oz	2 tbsp
8 oz	1 cup

Sugar

Caster/granulated or soft brown/dark brown

1 oz	2 tbsp
8 oz	1 cup

Icing/Confectioner's (sifted first)

1 oz	¼ cup
2 oz	under ½ cup
3 oz	⅔ cup
4 oz	¾ cup
6 oz	1 cup
8 oz	1⅔ cups
12 oz	2½ cups
1 lb	3⅓ cups

Yeast

½ oz dried	1 packet active dried

Selected Terminology

BRITISH	AMERICAN
Apples, cooking	Green apples
Bicarbonate of soda	Baking soda
Cherries, cooking	Tart or sour cherries
Coconut, desiccated	Flaked or grated coconut
Cornflour	Cornstarch
Cream, double	Whipping or heavy cream
Cream, single	Light cream
Crystallised fruits	Candied fruits
Custard powder	Not available; use cornstarch, vanilla essence and yellow colouring (or packet vanilla pudding)
Glacé cherries	Candied cherries
Golden syrup	Not available; use light corn syrup
Hazelnuts	Cob nuts or filberts
Jam	Preserves
Jelly	Jello
Marrow	Large zucchini
Rice, round grain	Short grain rice
Semolina	Semolina flour (not readily available, use farina)
Sugar	
Caster or granulated	Granulated
Soft brown	Light brown
Demerara	Light brown
Icing	Confectioners'
Sultanas	Seedless white raisins
Syrup, golden	Not available; use light corn syrup
Treacle	Molasses
Wholemeal	Whole wheat

Index

A

Abernethy Biscuits 158
Acton, Eliza, *Modern Cookery* 13, 99
Almond: Cake 100; Paste 168; Shortbread 150
Apple Cake: Dorset 28, 102; Somerset 104
Apple Potato Cakes, Irish 23
Ashbourne Gingerbread 66

B

Bachelor's Buttons 158
Bakestone: Fruit Scones 32; Tart, Welsh 32
Balmoral Cake 76
Banbury Cakes 131
Bannock, Pitcaithly 150; Selkirk 43
Bara Brith 84
Barham, R 70
Bath Buns 37
Battenburg Cake 123
Bedfordshire Wigs 146
Berwick May Day Tarts 135
Birds' Nests, Somerset 132
Biscuits: Abernethy 158; Caraway Lemon 154; Chocolate Bourbon 153; Digestive 154; Golf 160; Little Hollow 164; Rout 163; Savill Ginger 157
Black Bun 80
Blackmore Vale Hunt Cake 92
Boiled Cake; Gemma's 94; Miss Pedelty's Fruit 94; Wartime 93
Bosworth Jumbles 152
Bourbon Biscuits, Chocolate 153
Brandy Snaps 140
Bread: Caraway Seed 41; Yule 46
Bread Pudding 88
Brontë, Charlotte 96
Broonie, Orkney 60
Bun, Black 80
Buns: Bath 37; Caraway 42; Chelsea 38; Hot Cross 40; Raspberry 142; Revel 38
Bunyard, Lorna 96
Bury Simnel Cake 78
Butter: Cream 168; Tarts, Welsh 136
Butterfly Cakes 141
Buttermilk Cake, Cumberland 87
Byron, May 143

C

Caraway: Buns 42; Lemon Biscuits 154; Lemon Cake 98; Seed Bread 41
Caramel Icing for Cornflour Cake 118
Carol Singing Pepper Cake 62
Cattern Cakes 142
Celebration Cake 77
Cheese Scones 25
Cheesecakes: Curd 129; Welsh 130
Chelsea Buns 38
Cherry Cake 102
Chocolate: Bourbon Biscuits 153; Cake, Dark 122; Rum Cake 121
Christmas Eve Wigs 145
Cider Cake, Somerset 103
Cider Cream Cake, Taunton 125
Clifton Puffs 136
Coconut Cake 101
Coffee Fudge Cake 124
Colchester Gingerbread 57
Cornflour Cake with Caramel Icing 118
Cornish: Fairings 155; Heavy Cake 31; Tettie Cake 29
Courting Cake, Cumberland 134
Coventry Godcakes 135
Cowper, William 4
Cream Cake: Hunmany 32; Taunton Cider 125; West Country 84
Cumberland: Buttermilk Cake 87; Courting Cake 134; Currant Cake 130
Curd Cheesecakes 129

D

Dark Chocolate Cake 122
Date and Seed Cake 74
Date Slices 159
Deebank Sultana Cake 92
Defoe, Daniel 10
Digestive Biscuits 154
Dorset Apple Cake 28, 102
Dough Cake, Victorian 46
Doughnuts 50; Isle of Wight 51
Dripping Cake, Wholemeal 104
Drop Scones 26
Drops, Hampshire 112
Duke of Windsor Gingerbread 58
Dundee Cake 80

E

Easter Cakes: Sedgemoor 162; Shrewsbury 152, 162
Eccles Cakes 132
Eccles Wake Song 127

F

Fair Buttons: Norfolk Brown 164; Norfolk White 161
Fairings, Cornish 155

Fairy Cakes 141
Fat Rascals 29
Fig Cake, Palm Sunday 89
Fine Shortbread 150
Fingers, Sponge 111
Fishguard Gingerbread 61
Fitzwilliam, Countess 54
Flapjacks 161
Flead Cakes, Kentish 128
Fluffy Frosting, Walnut Cake with 120
Fochabers Gingerbread 61
Fruit: Scones 25; Bakestone 32
Fruit Cake: Marmalade 84; Miss Pedelty's Boiled 94; Tray 76
Fruit Spice Cake 72
Fudge Cake, Coffee 124

G

Gemma's Boiled Cake 94
Geranium Sponge 113
Gilbert, W.S. 35
Ginger Biscuits, Savill 157
Ginger Cake 62; Norfolk 64; Schoolboy's 68; Scot's 65
Ginger: Loaf 66; Nuts 156; Parkins 156; Shortbread 150, 156
Gingers, Norfolk 157
Gingerbread: Ashbourne 66; Colchester 57; Duke of Windsor 58; Fishguard 61; Fochabers 61; Grantham White 62; Grasmere 64; Inverness 58; Men 63; Old Welsh 59; Orange 59; Sticky 55
Gingerbreads, Grantham 64
Girdle Scones, Plain 24
Glacé Icing 167
Glasse, Hannah 143
Godcakes, Coventry 135
God's Kitchels 133
Golden Syrup Cake 66
Golf Biscuits 160
Goosnargh Cakes 146
Grantham: Gingerbreads 64; White Gingerbread 62
Granthams 159
Grasmere Gingerbread 64
Griddles, use of 22

H

Hampshire Drops 112
Harvest Betsy Cake 90
Harvest Cakes, Pembroke 45
Heavy Cake, Cornish 31
Highland Slim Cakes 30
Hollow Biscuits, Little 164
Honey Cake 56
Hot Cross Buns 40
Hunmanby Cream Cake 32

I

Icing: Glacé 167; Royal 169
Inverness Gingerbread 58
Irish: Johnny Cakes 139; Porter Cake 83; Potato Apple Cakes 23; Whiskey Cake 88
Isle of Wight Doughnuts 51

J

Jekyll, Lady 160
Johnny Cakes, Irish 139
Jumbles: Bosworth 152; Orange 160; Raspberry 158

K

Kentish Flead Cakes 128
Kettilby, Mary 70
Kitchels, God's 133

L

Lady Clark of Tillypronie 91
Lady Savill's Plain Luncheon Cake 92
Lamb, Charles 7
Lancashire Cakes 49
Lardy Cake 47
Lemon Caraway: Biscuits 154; Cake 98
Lincolnshire Whitsun Cake 48
Little Hollow Biscuits 164
Loaf: Ginger 66; Seed 97
Luncheon Cake 90; Lady Savill's Plain 92

M

Macaroons 140
Madeira Cake 106
Maids of Honour, Richmond 128
Mansfield, Katherine 54, 117
Marble Cake 98
Marmalade: Cake 101; Fruit Cake 84
May Bryon's Portugal Cakes 144
May Day Tarts, Berwick 135
Marzipan 168
Melting Moments 144
Middleton, C.H. 10
Miss Pedelty's Boiled Fruit Cake 94

N

Norfolk: Brown Fair Buttons 164; Ginger Cake 64; Gingers 157; Shortcake 134; White Fair Buttons 161
North Country Overnight Spice Cake 60
Northumberland Twists 52
Nuts, Ginger 156

O

Oast Cakes 52
Oatcakes 28
Oaten: Shortbread 152; Tea Scones 25
Old-Fashioned Plum Cake 73
Old Welsh Gingerbread 59
Orange: Gingerbread 59; Jumbles 160; Walnut Cake 105
Orkney Broonie 60
Overnight Spice Cake, North Country 60

P

Palm Sunday Fig Cake 89
Parkin: Sponge 67; Yorkshire 56
Parkins, Ginger 156
Parlies 68
Pastry: Puff 170; Shortcrust 170
Pembroke Harvest Cakes 45
Pepper Cake, Carol Singing 62
Petticoat Tails 151
Pickering, Henry 15
Picnic Cake 72
Pineapple Walnut Cake 100
Pitcaithly Bannock 150
Plain Girdle Scones 24
Plat, Sir Hugh 54
Plum Cake, Old-Fashioned 73
Plum Heavies, Sussex 27
Porter Cake, Irish 83
Portugal Cakes 143; May Byron's 144
Potato: Apple Cakes, Irish 23; Scones 23
Pratie Oaten 24
Proust, Marcel 7
Prune Cake 74
Pudding, Bread 88
Puff Pastry 170
Puffs: Almond 145; Chocolate 145; Clifton 136; Lemon 145

Q

Queen Cakes 141

R

Raisin Cake 73
Raspberry: Buns 142; Jumbles 158
Ratafias 163
Revel Buns 38
Richmond Maids of Honour 128
Rock Cakes 139
Roll, Swiss 114
Rout Biscuits 163
Royal Icing 169
Rum Chocolate Cake 121

S

Saffron Cake 44
Sally Lunn 42
Sand Cake 98
Sand Cakes 164
Sandwich, Victoria Sponge 114
Savill Ginger Biscuits 157
Savoy Cake 112
School Cake 75
Schoolboy's Ginger Cake 68
Scones: 24; Bakestone Fruit 32; Cheese 25; Drop 26; Fruit 25; Oaten Tea 25; Plain Girdle 24; Potato 23; Treacle 26
Scots' Ginger Cake 65
Scratching Cake 85
Scripture Cake 82
Sedgemoor Easter Cakes 162
Seed: and Date Cake 74; Cake 106; Loaf 97
Selkirk Bannock 43
Shakespeare, William 117
Shearing Cake, Welsh 108
Shilling Cake 74
Shortbread: Almond 150; Fine 150; Ginger 150, 156; Oaten 152; Three-Two-One 150
Shortcake, Norfolk 134
Shortcrust Pastry 170
Shrewsbury Easter Cakes 152, 162
Shropshire Soul Cakes 50
Simnel Cake 78; Bury 78
Singin' Hinny 26
Slices, Date 159
Slim Cakes, Highland 30
Snaps, Brandy 140
Soda Cake 99
Somerset: Apple Cake 104; Birds' Nests 132; Cider Cake 103
Soul Cakes, Shropshire 50
Spenser, Edmund 110
Spice Cake, North Country Overnight 60
Splits, West Country 39
Sponge Fingers 111; Geranium 113; Parkin 67; Sandwich, Victoria 114; Whisked 111
Stern, G.B. 148
Sticky Gingerbread 55
Sultana Cake, Deebank 92
Sussex Plum Heavies 27
Swiss Roll 114

T

Tart, Welsh Bakestone 32
Tarts: Berwick May Day 135; Welsh Butter 136
Taunton Cider Cream Cake 125
Teacakes 41
Tea Scones, Oaten 25
Teisen Lap 30
Tennis Cake 119
Tennyson, Alfred 138
Tettie Cake, Cornish 29
Thompson, Flora 35
Three-Two-One, Shortbread 150
Tray Fruit Cake 76
Treacle Scones 26
Twelfth Night Cake 86
Twists, Northumberland 52

Victoria Sponge Sandwich 114
Victorian Dough Cake 46
Vinegar Cake 86

W

Waffles 165
Walnut: and Pineapple Cake 100; Cake with Fluffy Frosting 120; Orange Cake 105
Wartime Boiled Cake 93
Welsh: Bakestone Tart 32; Cakes 30; Cheesecakes 130; Shearing Cake 108; Tarts, Butter 136
West Country: Cream Cake 84; Splits 39
Whisked Sponge 111
Whiskey Cake, Irish 88
Whitsun Cake, Lincolnshire 48
Wholemeal Dripping Cake 104
Wigs: Bedfordshire 146; Christmas Eve 145; Yeast 48

Yeast Wigs 48
Yorkshire Parkin 56
Yule Bread 46